DO I HAVE TO GO?

DO I HAVE TO GO?

101 QUESTIONS ABOUT THE MASS, THE EUCHARIST, AND YOUR SPIRITUAL LIFE

MATTHEW PINTO AND CHRIS STEFANICK

ASCENSION PRESS

West Chester, Pennsylvania

Nihil obstat: Rev. Robert A. Pesarchick, S.T.D.
            Censor Librorum
            January 31, 2008

Imprimatur: +Justin Cardinal Rigali
            Archbishop of Philadelphia
            January 31, 2008

Ascension Press
Post Office Box 1990
West Chester, PA 19380
Orders: 1-800-376-0520
www.AscensionPress.com

Cover design: Faceout Studio

Printed in the United States of America
11 12 13 8 7 6 5 4 3

ISBN 978-1-934217-33-7

To our parents, who gave us life, raised us on
the bread of life, and always made us go!

Dear young people, the happiness you are seeking,
the happiness you have a right to enjoy has a name and a face:
It is Jesus of Nazareth, hidden in the Eucharist.

– Pope Benedict XVI, World Youth Day 2005

We declare to you what was from the beginning, what we have heard,
what we have seen with our eyes, what we have looked at and touched
with our hands, concerning the word of life …
So that you also may have fellowship with us …
So that our joy may be complete.

– 1 John 1:1, 3-4

CONTENTS

Key to Biblical Abbreviations

The following abbreviations are used for the various Scriptural verses cited throughout the book. (*Note:* CCC = *Catechism of the Catholic Church.*)

Old Testament

Gn	Genesis	Jon	Jonah
Ex	Exodus	Mi	Micah
Lv	Leviticus	Na	Nahum
Nm	Numbers	Hb	Habakkuk
Dt	Deuteronomy	Zep	Zephaniah
Jos	Joshua	Hg	Haggai
Jgs	Judges	Zec	Zechariah
Ru	Ruth	Mal	Malachi
1 Sam	1 Samuel		
2 Sam	2 Samuel		
1 Kgs	1 Kings	**New Testament**	
2 Kgs	2 Kings	Mt	Matthew
1 Chr	1 Chronicles	Mk	Mark
2 Chr	2 Chronicles	Lk	Luke
Ezr	Ezra	Jn	John
Neh	Nehemiah	Acts	Acts
Tb	Tobit	Rom	Romans
Jdt	Judith	1 Cor	1 Corinthians
Est	Esther	2 Cor	2 Corinthians
1 Mc	1 Maccabees	Gal	Galatians
2 Mc	2 Maccabees	Eph	Ephesians
Jb	Job	Phil	Philippians
Ps	Psalms	Col	Colossians
Prv	Proverbs	1 Thess	1 Thessalonians
Eccl	Ecclesiastes	2 Thess	2 Thessalonians
Sng	Song of Songs	1 Tm	1 Timothy
Wis	Wisdom	2 Tm	2 Timothy
Sir	Sirach	Ti	Titus
Is	Isaiah	Phlm	Philemon
Jer	Jeremiah	Heb	Hebrews
Lam	Lamentations	Jas	James
Bar	Baruch	1 Pt	1 Peter
Ez	Ezekiel	2 Pt	2 Peter
Dn	Daniel	1 Jn	1 John
Hos	Hosea	2 Jn	2 John
Jl	Joel	3 Jn	3 John
Am	Amos	Jude	Jude
Ob	Obadiah	Rv	Revelation

INTRODUCTION

The history of the Catholic faith is filled with stories of heroism. Over the past two-thousand years, many Catholics have stood before kings and defended their faith—and embraced the crosses that came as a result. Many even suffered martyrdom, while millions of others suffered persecution for their steadfast beliefs. As recently as this past Sunday, thousands of Catholics in Muslim and Communist countries risked their freedom and even their lives to attend Mass and receive Our Lord in the Holy Eucharist. Indeed, the history of Christianity reveals that attendance at Mass, in particular, has often been the final act of faith in the lives of countless heroic men and women.

Today, however, a great number of Catholics, upon waking up on a Sunday morning, ask the age-old question, "Do I really have to go?" And many who do go to Mass, instead of entering into the "active participation" in the liturgy that the Church calls for, daydream about what they will do after—from the sports they will watch or play, to the housework they need to get done, or to the movie they will go see that evening. Others, in increasing numbers, simply decide not to go to Mass at all.

What do those Catholics who risk martyrdom to attend Mass know that millions of their fellow believers today seem to miss—or, worse, are indifferent to? What could they possibly have found in this ancient collection of prayers and rituals that is actually worth dying for?

They must have discovered the sublime truth about which *Lord of the Rings* author and devout Catholic J.R.R. Tolkien so eloquently writes: "Out of the darkness of my life, so much frustrated, I put before you the one great thing to love on earth: the Blessed Sacrament ... There you will find romance, glory, honor, fidelity, and the true way of all your loves upon earth." In other words, they found something at Mass that satisfies the insatiable desire of the human heart for love, truth, and meaning—something that gaining all the wealth of the world cannot satisfy.

As converts from a "Do I have to go?" attitude to a "I really want to go" conviction, the authors of this book have experienced the glimmer of heaven that the Mass was created to be. By God's grace, we have experienced a little of what Sts. Peter, John, and James did on the summit of Mount Tabor at the Transfiguration, and we have wanted to remain there in the presence of our loving God.

It is because of our belief in the power of the Eucharist and the Mass that we have sought to address some of the common questions young people have about how we are to worship God. As most Catholic youth do today, we had a lot of questions as we grew in the faith—and still do. This short book is our attempt to pass on some of what we have learned so you may get there faster than we did. We do not claim that the answers in this book will satisfy in any manner close to what the Mass will. Why? Because the awesome mystery of God cannot be summed up in questions and answers.

God is a Person—actually, three Persons, the Holy Trinity—and the Mass is a firsthand experience of that Person, the Maker of the Universe, pouring Himself out for and into us. At the Mass, God presents Himself as someone to be "seen with our eyes ... looked at and touched with our hands" (1 Jn 1:1).

The saints throughout history made this intimate encounter with God in the Eucharist the source and summit of their lives. Spiritually fed by God Himself, they found in the Mass the power to begin to live as God lives—fused with love and holiness. They tapped into the mystery of who God *is*, releasing the power to become fully who they are—fully human and fully alive! The "secret" of the saints is really no more complex than that. They were "powered" by the Eucharist.

Have you ever wondered why people who live near some of the most amazing tourist destinations in the world never go to see them? For example, the majority of New Yorkers have never been to the Empire State Building or to the Statue of Liberty, and most Hawaiians never break out surf boards to experience the exhilaration of riding some of the best waves on the planet. Why is this? Simply because they are busy with the concerns and demands of daily life.

In the Mass, we have the best destination in the universe within our reach. The waters of God's grace surround us. At Mass, we do not just talk about heaven, we actually get a taste of it. In the Eucharistic sacrifice, we are surrounded by angels, saints, and loved ones who have passed into eternal bliss, separated only by a thin veil and listening to the voice of God with us. At Mass we do not just remember the cross and resurrection; they are actually made present to us in a sacramental way.

It is our hope and prayer that this book will help you to kick off your shoes and dive into the ocean of grace that is the Mass with all your heart, mind, and strength! If you do, your life will never be the same again.

—Matthew Pinto and Chris Stefanick

Chapter 1

WORSHIP 101

1. Why do I have to worship God?

When we worship God we are acknowledging our absolute dependence on Him for our existence, our life, and our ultimate and eternal happiness. God is the loving source of everything that exists. He not only created you and me out of love, but sustains our existence in that same love at every moment of our lives: "In him we live and move and have our being" (Acts 17:26-28).

God created us in order that we may share in His divine life. In this knowledge, we should rejoice and give thanks to God for all that He desires to give us. As St. Augustine, speaking of God, said, "You have made us for yourself, and our hearts are restless until they rest in you."[1] In this, we come to the realization of the true meaning and purpose of our lives—union with God.

This union begins in our worship of Him. Worship of God helps us avoid turning in on ourselves, which can lead to sin and an unhealthy attachment to the things of this world. Worship is expressed in our sacrificial offerings to God, in our humble prayer of surrender, praise, and gratitude. We do this especially at Mass, when we offer our lives to the Father through Jesus and receive all that He

did for us. It is also expressed in a *lifestyle* of worship—
that is, a lifestyle that acknowledges God and puts Him
first. This kind of lifestyle is liberating and challenging.
When we fail to worship God we start putting all sorts
of other things in His place, making them our "gods."
The first commandment forbids idolatry, the worship
of false gods. Worship of the one true God is necessary
for an "integrated" life and saves us from the "endless
disintegration" that comes from chasing one false god after
another (see CCC 2114).

Worship is not only a prerequisite for holiness and
happiness; it is also a matter of justice (which is giving to
others what is owed to them). Just as children owe their
parents honor, obedience, and respect because of all that
their parents have done for them, even more so we owe
God reverence as a way of acknowledging all He has done
for us. To be indifferent to God, the One whom we can
thank for the gift of our very existence, is seriously sinful.

That being said, the more mature a relationship is (whether
with God or one's parents), the more one is able to respond
lovingly as justice demands and not simply out of a sense
of obligation. Therefore, we worship God because: 1)
worshiping Him helps transform us into holy and happy
people; 2) in justice, we owe God our worship, since He
created and redeemed us; and 3) we love Him.

2.   How do we know that God even exists?

Over the centuries, a number of philosophers and
theologians have offered various arguments (also
known as "proofs") for the existence of God. The most
notable among these thinkers is St. Thomas Aquinas
(1225–1274), who developed five "cosmological" proofs for

God's existence. One of these arguments is known as the argument from "design." We wouldn't look at a book and assume that it has no author. An intelligible creation such as a book implies an intelligent creator. Well, the universe is far more complex and orderly than any book. According to St. Thomas, common sense shows us that the order in the universe demonstrates that it was designed by an intelligent designer, i.e., God. In other words, all physical laws and the order of nature and life were decreed and designed by God, the intelligent designer.[2]

Distinguished biologist Edwin Conklin, an associate of Albert Einstein at Princeton University, agrees with St. Thomas: "The probability of life originating from an accident is comparable to the probability of the unabridged dictionary resulting from an explosion in a print shop."[3]

God may have created the world through a "big bang" followed by millions of years of evolution, or He may have simply created everything at once in its current form. We do not know for sure. What is certain, however, is that it is absolutely illogical to look at an intelligently ordered and beautiful creation—a book, a painting, a tree, or a fingernail—and deny that an intelligent creator is behind it.

3.   To be honest, I have a hard time believing in God because of all the suffering in the world.

Actually, this is a common objection that many people raise in questioning God's goodness or even His very existence. There seems to be an obvious contradiction between a God who is Love and the existence of suffering. As the *Catechism of the Catholic Church* notes, "The world we live in often seems very far from the one promised us by faith.

Our experiences of evil and suffering, injustice, and death, seem to contradict the Good News; they can shake our faith and become a temptation against it" (CCC 164).

Our Catholic faith, though, offers a compelling insight into the problem of suffering: As a result of original sin, we live in an imperfect world. God only *permits* suffering, while intending to bring about a greater good through it, a good which sometimes can be grasped only from the perspective of eternity. The crucifixion and death of Jesus is perhaps the best example of this truth. God allowed the suffering—and murder—of His only-begotten Son to save us from our sins. This profound suffering led to the resurrection, brought us our salvation, and taught the world what love is, and the dignity of every human person.

Of course, when we are in the midst of suffering, we may have little patience with theological explanations. The best thing to do in such times is to look at the Cross. When we consider Jesus' suffering and death on the Cross, we realize that God has not promised us that our lives will be comfortable and prosperous in a worldly sense. We see a God who says, "life may be really, really difficult sometimes ... but I am with you."[4]

This message is conveyed to us loud and clear in the Eucharist. Face-to-face with Jesus in the Eucharist—the enduring sign of His body, broken for us—we can never say to God, "you don't know what it is like to deal with pain, suffering, rejection, and death"... because He does. (Nor can we claim that we love Him and then be indifferent to those in our world who are weak, because He has made Himself one of them.[5]) And He is with us, no matter how tough things might get in life, even to the end.

4.   How do we know that Jesus is God?

Because He said so—and to prove it He worked miracles
and rose from the dead.

Some people, rejecting His divinity, like to reduce Jesus to
being merely a "great prophet" or "wise man," i.e., a good
man who taught us a better way to live. The problem with
this view is that Jesus *claimed* to be divine throughout the
gospels. As C. S. Lewis has pointed out, if a man claims to
be God, he is either a liar, a lunatic, or truly God.[6] "Wise
man" is no longer an option. Jesus' claim to be God was
the main reason He was put to death. Looking at Jesus'
life, we can see that He demonstrated His divinity by His
actions, in particular by the many miracles He performed.
Thus, "liar" and "lunatic" can be safely ruled out, leaving
us with only one logical conclusion—He is God.

No other founder of a major world religion rose from
the dead to prove his divinity; in fact, none of them ever
even claimed to be divine. In the nineteenth century,
distinguished Harvard law professor Dr. Simon Greenleaf
set out to prove that Jesus' resurrection would never hold
up in a court of law. Looking at the evidence, Greenleaf
noted the great number of eyewitnesses to the resurrection
who were willing to die rather than retract their testimony.
All of the apostles, with the exception of St. John (who
died in exile), were put to death for preaching the Gospel,
specifically about the resurrection of Jesus. Greenleaf
concluded that these were not people dying for some vague
belief but for a specific event that they had witnessed. His
verdict? He became a Christian![7]

This means that while other religions may have glimpses
of the truth about who God is, we can find the fullness of

truth about God in Jesus Christ—who is God in the flesh, personally showing us that He is love.

5. What is the Mass?

According to the *Catechism*, the Mass is the "source and summit of the Christian life" (CCC 1324). In other words, our faith has its beginning ("source") and highest expression ("summit") in the celebration of the Holy Eucharist. All of the other sacraments and all other Christian ministries are linked with the Mass and are oriented toward it (see CCC 1324). This is an awesome mystery. A few words of explanation are needed to unpack it.

At the Last Supper, on the night before He died, Jesus took bread, blessed it, broke it, and gave it to His disciples saying, "Take and eat. This is my body which is given up for you." He also took a cup and shared it with them saying, "Take and drink. This is my blood which is poured out for you." He then told His apostles, the first bishops, "Do this in remembrance of me" (see Lk 22:14-20). From its very beginning, the Church has been faithful to this command of Jesus by celebrating the Mass (see CCC 1342).

The Mass is more than just a memorial; it is a "re-presentation" of Jesus' sacrifice on the Cross, making it "present" for us here and now (CCC 1366). Jesus left us the gift of the Mass because it was not enough for Him that His followers should just hear about His saving death, resurrection, and ascension. He wanted all of His disciples in every generation until the end of time to "take and eat," and have a direct encounter with His very body, blood, soul, and divinity in the Eucharist. As Pope Benedict XVI has written, "In the Eucharist Jesus does not give us a 'thing,' but

Himself; He offers His own body and pours out His own blood. He gives us the totality of His life."[8]

The two main parts of the Mass are: 1) the *Liturgy of the Word*, in which we hear readings from the Scriptures proclaimed, listen to a homily explaining and applying these readings to our lives, and pray intercessory prayers; and 2) the *Liturgy of the Eucharist*, in which bread and wine are brought to the altar and, through the prayer of consecration, become the very body and blood of Christ, who we receive in Holy Communion (see CCC 1346).

The Mass is considered both a "sacrificial memorial" and a "sacred banquet." The "altar of sacrifice" at the Mass can also be called the "table of the Lord," around which the entire Church on earth gathers to join the Church in heaven in celebrating and feasting on the gift of redemption (CCC 1382–1383).

Incidentally, the English word "Mass" is derived from the Latin *missa*, which comes from the same root as the word *missio* ("mission"). God empowers and sends us out from the Mass on a mission to be like Christ for the world: to love others as He has loved us (see Jn 13:1-15).[9]

6.   Why should I go to Mass?

We humans, with our ability to *know* and to *love*, are more than a random by-product of a cosmic explosion; we are more than just "evolved animals." An intelligent Creator designed us for a purpose: to know, love, and serve Him in this life and to be happy with Him forever in the next. Despite what the commercial says, all the Snickers in the world won't make us "really satisfied"—and neither will all the money, success, power, pleasure, or popularity. Only living out our purpose will. In the words of St. Augustine quoted earlier, "You have made us for yourself, O Lord, and our hearts are restless until they rest in you."[10] Only the God who made us—and for whom we were made—can fill our hearts with the peace and love we long for.

In the Mass, God gives us the only thing that makes us "really satisfied": His very self.[11] While we can and do encounter God in other ways—for instance, through prayer, reading the Bible, or serving others—all of these actions point to and are enlivened by our reception of Jesus, body, blood, soul, and divinity, in the Eucharist. Just as food strengthens and sustains our bodies, the Eucharist nourishes us spiritually by uniting us with the risen Christ (see CCC 1392).

So the Mass is the richest encounter we can have with God this side of eternity. It helps us fulfill the core purpose of our existence: union with the God we were made for. Only by being united with Him can we truly know and love Him—and truly serve Him by loving others with His own divine love. Because it fuels us to live out our purpose (i.e., knowing, loving, and serving God), the Mass gives us the grace we need to live life "to the full" (see Jn 10:10)—not just an average human life, but a life full of grace, which is a share in the inner life of God Himself. This life of holiness is the life we were created to live. Any other kind of life, no matter how successful it may seem, is a failure in the ultimate sense—a failure to live out our very purpose. Anything less is empty.

Finally, we should at least attend Mass every Sunday because God, knowing us and our needs better than we know ourselves, commands us to. (See the third commandment and Jesus' command at the Last Supper to "do this in remembrance of me"). So, unless we have an urgent reason to disregard God's straightforward command, it is foolish not to heed His words.

7. So what happens to us at Mass?

When we attend Mass, we encounter God and thereby are united with Him and sanctified, i.e., made holy. Since everyone is called to holiness, this is a good thing. Contrary to popular misconceptions, holiness does not make us "weird" or our lives boring; rather, it makes us more fully who we are, more fully alive. Jesus said "I came so that they might have life, and have it to the full" (Jn 10:10). Mass makes us holy by letting us experience the Word of God, uniting us to Jesus in the Eucharist, uniting us to the Church (His Mystical Body on earth), and strengthening us to share in Jesus' mission to the world.

When we hear God's Word proclaimed at Mass, we come to know Him. St. Jerome said, "Ignorance of Scripture is ignorance of Christ."[12] A knowledge of Sacred Scripture lies at the foundation of forming a relationship with Him, imitating Him, and thus pleasing Him and thereby becoming more fully ourselves.

When we receive the Eucharist, we receive the grace to live out God's will in our lives. Our souls, like our bodies, need nourishment to grow and be strengthened for the demands of daily life. Receiving Jesus in the Eucharist provides this nourishment. The Eucharist is as essential to life in Christ as food is necessary for life in the body (CCC 1391). As Jesus Himself said, "He who eats me will live because of me" (Jn 6:57).

At Mass we also experience and become part of the deep communion that is the Church. As the *Catechism* states, "The Eucharist makes the Church" (CCC 1396). One beautiful title for the Church is "the Mystical body of Christ." By uniting each individual more fully to Himself in the Eucharist, Christ unites us more deeply to one another, making us one body in Him. There is no deeper fellowship than this. So, in short, the Eucharist also unifies and strengthens God's earthly family—the Church—so we can carry out His mission of truth and justice together.

When we go to Mass we are sent on a mission from God to our world, to our families, to our workplaces, and to our circle of friends to build up the Kingdom of God there. As mentioned earlier, the word "Mass" in Latin, *missa* ("dismissal"), is derived from the *missio*, which means "mission." God did not accomplish all this for us so we could keep it to ourselves, but so we could share His mission of building the Kingdom. When we encounter Jesus, alive and well in the Eucharist, we should be like the apostles, standing in awe before the empty tomb. They encountered a love, hope, and power that was far too great to keep them themselves. They had to share it! Likewise, the love that Christ gives us in the Eucharist is far too great to keep to ourselves. The dismissal (*missa*) from Mass is "a starting point" for our mission to share, not just a way of life, but the person of Jesus Christ with the entire world.[13]

The Eucharist empowers us to recognize and serve Jesus in the poor (CCC 1397) and anyone in need, with whom Jesus intimately associates Himself (see Mt 25:31-46). Blessed Pier Giorgio Frassatti, a Catholic young adult who went to daily Mass and served the poor every day, often said, "Christ comes to visit me in the Holy Eucharist; I repay the visit by going to find Him in the poor." As Blessed Teresa of Calcutta, who devoted her entire life to service of the poorest of the poor, has said, "The Mass is the spiritual food that sustains me—without which I could not get through one single day or hour in my life." At the Mass, God gives us the same grace He gave the saints to become holy and to sanctify the world around us. We simply need to cooperate with that grace through a life of prayer, virtue, and service/mission.

8.   **What is the difference between the Mass and my Protestant friend's Sunday worship service?**

In a word, "sacrifice." Let us explain.

All Christians—Catholics, Orthodox, and Protestants alike—agree that the primary reason we attend church on Sunday is to worship God, fulfilling the third commandment to "Remember the Sabbath day, to keep it holy" (Ex 20:8; Dt 5:12). Where we disagree is what form this worship should take. While many Protestant Sunday services are often dynamic and exciting, filled with great music and preaching, they do not reflect the way the liturgy was celebrated in the earliest days of the Church. Even those Protestant communities which have a "higher" liturgical tradition (e.g., Lutherans, Anglicans)—whose form of worship somewhat resembles the Catholic Mass— lack certain essential elements, e.g., a valid priesthood, the Real Presence of Christ in the Eucharist, etc.

Here's the background: The Christian faith was born out of the faith of ancient Hebrews, God's chosen people to whom He revealed Himself so as to prepare the world for the coming of the Messiah. Therefore, we can find a continuity and completion of the Jewish tradition in Christianity, which was established by Christ upon the apostles. This is especially true when it comes to the themes of redemption, sacrifice, and worship.

By divine command, sacrifice was at the center of the worship of the Jewish people. In Old Testament times the people offered sacrifice to God in atonement for (i.e., to make up for) their sins, as a pledge of their commitment to Him, and to offer Him adoration. Specific sacrifices were prescribed for various occasions. These sacrifices, offered daily, were completed and replaced by the one sacrifice of Jesus Christ on the Cross (see Heb 10). His sacrifice was the perfect sacrifice which solidifies our covenant with God, pays the price for all sin, and is the perfect act of worship to God the Father. As it was in the Old Testament, so in the New, sacrifice remains at the center of worship when we fulfill Jesus' command to "do this in remembrance of me" at Mass.

We do not claim to sacrifice Jesus again and again at every Mass. As St. Paul said, Jesus was sacrificed "once for all" (Heb 10:10). His sacrifice is mystically "re-presented" for us at every Mass in an "unbloody manner" (CCC 1366). In the Mass, the curtain of time is torn open and we stand at the foot of the Cross as Jesus pours out His life for us. As the *Catechism* notes, "The sacrifice of Christ and the sacrifice of the Eucharist are one single sacrifice" (CCC 1367). This is why the Church has always referred to the "Holy *Sacrifice* of the Mass."

God did this so that every generation until the end of time could have an immediate, tangible, and real connection to the Cross and its healing power, which is manifested in Our Lord's resurrection and Ascension (which are also called to mind and experienced at every Eucharist). In the words of St. Augustine, we "receive in this bread that which was hanged on the cross; [and] receive in this cup that which was poured from Christ's side." In other words, "Take and eat, this is My body, which is given up [i.e., handed over, scourged, crowned with thorns, suspended on the Cross for three hours, killed by asphyxiation] for you." When we recognize and give our "Amen" to what He did for us, even receiving it physically, this is true worship—a recognition of who God is and who we are before Him.

And as this sacrifice is re-presented in our midst, we are supposed to join in the priest's prayers in our hearts, giving our "Amen" to Jesus' self-offering to God the Father as "the great high priest" (Heb 4:14) on our behalf. When the priest (who participates in Christ's priesthood) holds up Jesus, and the whole Church joins this prayer of offering, we are taking part in the perfect offering of Jesus on the Cross. There is no more perfect sacrifice or act of worship than this.

Protestants do not believe in this kind of worship, nor could they offer it even if they did. Jesus said "do this in remembrance of me" to the apostles, who passed this authority on to their successors, the bishops. In order to be able to consecrate the Eucharist, one needs to be ordained by a bishop whose authority was handed down from bishop to bishop since the days of the apostles. This is known as "apostolic succession." Unfortunately, Protestants, who broke away from the Catholic Church five hundred years ago, do not have a valid sacramental priesthood.

While, on a human level, some Protestant Sunday services may appear to be more "exciting" than the Mass, this is judging by a faulty standard. Certainly God wants us to have great preaching and great music, but these are secondary to the sacrifice that should be at the heart of true Christian worship. This sacrifice can be found only in Catholic and Orthodox liturgies.

9.   **But didn't the Catholic Church invent the Mass? Certainly this is not the way the early Christians would have worshiped.**

No, the Catholic Church did not invent the Mass. Though the manner in which the Mass is celebrated has developed since the time of the apostles, the basic structure and the essential elements were given to us by Jesus and are rooted in Old Testament tradition. This is reflected in the following Gospel accounts of the Last Supper:

> When the hour came, he took his place at table with the apostles. He said to them, "I have eagerly desired to eat this Passover with you before I suffer ... Then he took a loaf of bread, and when he had given thanks, he broke it and gave it to them, saying, "This is my body, which is given for you. Do this in remembrance of me." And he did the same with the cup after supper, saying, "This cup that is poured out for you is the new covenant in my blood" (Lk 22:14-15, 19-20).

> While they were eating, Jesus took bread, said the blessing, broke it, and giving it to his disciples said, "Take and eat; this is my body." Then he took a cup, gave thanks, and gave it to them, saying, "Drink from it, all of you, for this is my blood of the new covenant, which will be shed on behalf of many for the forgiveness of sins" (Mt 26:26-30).

A similar account is found in Mark, chapter 14.

So, although particular aspects of the Mass—including the language in which it has been celebrated—have changed over the centuries, the central focus and essential elements of the Mass have stayed the same; the Church has remained faithful to Jesus' command at the Last Supper to "do this in remembrance of me."

10. **You mentioned that the Mass is "rooted in Old Testament tradition." What Old Testament tradition was Jesus celebrating at the Last Supper?**

At the Last Supper, Jesus was celebrating the Passover.

Sacrificial offerings made as an expression of worship can be seen throughout the Old Testament. The high point of Jewish worship, though, was (and remains) the Passover. The Passover commemorated how the Jewish people were set free from slavery in Egypt by the sacrifice of an unblemished lamb (see Ex 12:5). For those households who, in obedience to God (speaking through Moses), sacrificed a lamb, put its blood on their door, and ate its flesh, the angel of death "passed over" their homes and the lives of their firstborn sons were spared. In all other homes the firstborn son died. After this act of God, the Pharaoh released the Hebrews from slavery. Thus, the Passover sacrifice recalls how God led His people out of Egypt into freedom. As prescribed in the twelfth chapter of Exodus, the Jewish people were to sacrifice a lamb and eat it with unleavened bread as an offering to God in thanksgiving for what He had done and to commemorate this event every year.

At the Last Supper, as He was celebrating the Passover with His apostles, Jesus elevated and fulfilled the Old Testament tradition by "reveal[ing] that He himself is the *true* sacrificial lamb, destined in the Father's plan from the foundation of the world."[14] When He offered the unleavened bread and said to His apostles "this is my body," Jesus became the new Passover Lamb, the "Lamb of God" (see Jn 1:29), setting His people free from slavery to sin and death, and making them God's own children. As God promised, the sacrificial worship of Passover is fulfilled and continues to the end of time in the "perpetual institution" of the Mass (see Ex 12:14).

11. Why does God need all these rituals?

God doesn't need rituals—we do. Every culture throughout history attests to this fact. From the jungles of South America to the urban centers of Europe, all cultures have their social rituals, with ceremonies ranging from burial rites to birthday cakes to greetings, from handshakes to hugs. This is true regarding religious rituals as well. If, like the angels, we were pure spirits, we would simply worship God with our intellects and wills. However, since we are spirit and matter, soul and body, we need to encounter and express unseen realities in tangible, external ways.

The Church recognizes this and meets us where we are, using tangible signs to express unseen realities. The seven sacraments, for example, give us the grace (an unseen reality) that the ceremonial words and actions signify (see CCC 1131). Sacramentals, too, are signs of our worship and devotion to God—for example, making the sign of the cross, having statues of saints in our churches to remind us of the heavenly family that surrounds us, and blessing ourselves with holy water as we enter a church to remind us of our baptism. Just as a picture of our relatives helps remind us of a greater reality—our family—so too material things often assist us in understanding, appreciating, and experiencing greater things found in the spiritual realm.

Having created us, God also recognizes that we are composed of body and soul, and so He meets us where we are. He did so most remarkably by becoming incarnate (taking on human flesh). He also continues to let us encounter Him in tangible ways through the sacraments that He left to His Church.

12. **But doesn't all this "religion" get in the way of a genuine relationship with Jesus? My Evangelical friend claims that it does, and when I see so many people just going through the motions, I tend to agree.**

It depends on what you mean by "religion." If by "religion" you mean merely a set of rules and rituals invented by man, then the answer is certainly "yes." Such a religion could, indeed, come between us and God. If, however, you are talking about the true religion given to us by God Himself (i.e., the Catholic faith), along with the sacred rituals He has given us to make us holy and bring us closer to Him (i.e., the sacraments, including the Eucharist), the answer is a resounding "no." Jesus, the Son of God, told His apostles to celebrate Mass (see Lk 22:19) and to "make disciples of all nations, baptizing them in the name of the Father, and of the Son, and of the Holy Spirit" (Mt 28:19). Since every Christian tradition agrees on the need to celebrate baptism (though they have different understanding of its meaning), even your Evangelical friend would accept some "ritual" as part of Christianity.

Jesus left us rituals, especially the sacraments, to celebrate as a way to encounter Him and be filled with His grace. Married couples have various rituals such as candy on Valentine's Day, going to a particular restaurant on their anniversary, or flowers following an argument. People can fall into just going through the motions in marriage just as in faith. Would a marriage counselor propose that a couple whose relationship is on the rocks stop celebrating Valentine's Day? Not likely.

Likewise, although the Church recognizes that some may go to Mass without having Jesus at the center of their lives, she tirelessly works to evangelize them.[15] But the Church has never considered abandoning the sacraments that Jesus left us as a solution! That would be throwing the baby out with the bath water.

13. What exactly is a sacrament?

To paraphrase the *Catechism*, a sacrament is sign instituted by Christ to give us God's grace. It is covenant ritual in which we encounter Jesus in powerful and tangible ways. In each sacrament there is a symbol that becomes a reality. For example, in baptism a person goes into the water and comes out again. This is symbolic of going into the tomb with Christ and rising again with Him to new life. As this action is performed the transformation that is symbolized (dying to one's "old self" and rising to new life in Christ) actually happens, just as Scripture tells us it does (see Jn 3:5 and Acts 2:38, among others). The baptized person becomes a "new creation" (2 Cor 5:17).

In the sacrament of confirmation a person is anointed with oil which is a symbol of the Holy Spirit. At that moment, the Holy Spirit actually anoints that person in a new and deeper way. The bread and wine used at Mass symbolize the body and blood of Christ and they become what they symbolize: they actually become the body and blood of Christ (even though they keep the appearances of bread and wine).

God does not shun the material universe; after all, it is His creation. He didn't choose to be some distant cosmic reality that we need to put our spiritual antennas up to tune in to. He took matter (flesh) unto Himself. He has a face and a name, Jesus. He gave us the Church and the sacraments, and promised He would remain with us and in His Church until the end of time (see Mt 28:20; Jn 15:4-5; Eph 1:22; 1 Cor 12:27). In the Incarnation, He is a God we can see, hear, and touch. He is a God who meets us in our human condition, as bodily creatures.

Sacraments have been an essential part of the Church's life since its very beginning. In Acts 2, after Peter preaches to a crowd, they ask him the question that all preachers long to hear, "What then are we to do?" His response was: "be baptized" (Acts 2:38). This same passage concludes by saying that, "Those who accepted his message were baptized, and about three thousand persons were added that day" (Acts 2:38, 41). For two thousand years, the Church has continued this same practice. Those who heed the word of Christ, as taught to us by the Church, find in the sacraments the living Christ. As the *Catechism* beautifully says, it is the sacraments that "manifest and communicate to [us] ... the mystery of communion with the God who is love" (CCC 1118).

14. **I feel closer to God when I am outside, in nature. Why do I need to go to Mass to worship Him?**

You may indeed feel a deeper peace in the mountains than at Mass, and you may feel more inspired looking at the ocean than at a stained-glass window. That's fine, and even understandable. God created these things. They are distant "icons" (i.e., images) of Him that give us a glimpse of His beauty, vastness, and power.

If spending time outdoors nourishes your soul, then do it. Many of the saints did so. For example, Blessed Pier Giorgio Frasatti was an avid mountain climber, and St.

Francis of Assisi probably perceived God in nature more than anyone else in Christian history. Pope John Paul II loved to ski, hike, and kayak. He would even take religious retreats and spend a good part of the day skiing! But these holy men and women all spent much of their time in church, at daily Mass and praying before the Blessed Sacrament. They would be the first to agree that, while one may or may not have a grace-filled moment in nature, every Mass is guaranteed to be filled with the presence of God, even if we don't "feel" it.

God is present in four specific ways in the Mass:

1. *In His people.* God dwells in our hearts through baptism. With our ability to know (intellect) and love (free will), we image God in a profound way.

2. *In His priest.* Jesus Christ is present to us in a sacramental way through the person of the priest who, by virtue of the sacrament of holy orders, stands *in persona Christi* ("in the person of Christ").

3. *In the Scriptures.* Every time Sacred Scripture is proclaimed, God pours out His life-changing grace upon His people so that they can put this word into action. As the Second Vatican Council (1962-1965) proclaimed, "For in the sacred books, the Father who is in heaven meets His children with great love and speaks with them" (*Dei Verbum*, no. 21).

4. *In the Eucharist.* This is where we most fully and intensely encounter Jesus, who is truly present under the appearance of bread and wine—body, blood, soul, and divinity.

God may be *spiritually* present with you as you walk through the woods, but He is both spiritually and *physically* present during the Mass and in the tabernacle. So, if nature nourishes you spiritually, then by all means, spend some time praying there. But if you want to experience God in the deepest way possible in this life, go to Mass.

15. But why do we need to worship God with other people?

Communal worship flows from who God is, who He made us to be, and how He created His Church.

God is a communion of persons—the Trinity. The Father, Son, and Holy Spirit are three distinct Persons yet one God. Though it is an unfathomable mystery, the Trinity is a dogma of the faith, so we are bound to believe it. This Trinitarian God made us in His image and likeness (see Gn 1:26-27); thus, He did not create us to be alone. He made us to live in communion with others. This fact touches on every area of our lives, including family, work, sports, politics, and even worship. While it is crucial that we have a relationship with God that is deeply personal, it is also crucial that we have a relationship with Him that is communal. Because we are communal creatures, it would be "unnatural" for us to fail to offer God public, communal worship.

Communal worship also flows from the very nature of the Christian religion. Faith is a public matter. God did not just reveal Himself to you, redeem you, and call you into mission. He revealed Himself to everyone, redeemed a people, made us a family, and called us to partake in the mission of the Church to the whole world. A spirituality that is solely "one on one" can be egocentric, unhealthy, and misguided. ("It's just Jesus and me and to heck with thee!")

The Mass is the highest form of communal worship. At Mass we are united with one another in one act of worship, with the saints and our loved ones who have passed into the eternal and heavenly Liturgy (see CCC 1326, and question 56 for a definition of the term "liturgy"), and above all, with the Trinity as we offer ourselves to the Father, "through him (Jesus), with him, and in him, in the unity of the Holy Spirit" (prayer taken from the Mass).

16. I stopped going to Mass because there are so many hypocrites in my parish. Why should I worship with such people?

Reality check: There are going to be people who bother you everywhere you go. Does that mean you should stay home and never go to school, the movies, the grocery store, or work ever again? Of course not. So why stay home from Mass?

There has been hypocrisy in the Church (as in every institution that involves sinful human beings) since its beginning. We are all aware of the recent scandals in the Church involving a very small percentage of priests and bishops. (We always need to remember that the overwhelming majority of priests and bishops are good, dedicated men.) Scandals involving members of the clergy are nothing new. The apostles were the first bishops, and one of them caused extraordinary scandal—Judas, who betrayed Jesus for money and turned Him in to be killed. If you are counting, that is one (or 8.5%) out of twelve. Did the Jesus' other disciples then decide to turn away from Him and His teachings because of the "hypocrisy" of a Church leader? No, because they were not followers of Judas but of Christ. Judas did not hang on the Cross and die for them; Jesus did. Though it hurt them deeply, Judas' failure did not affect their faith in Jesus—nor in the Church that He had founded.

What did Judas' sin have to do with them and God? Nothing. Just so, the sinfulness and hypocrisy you may encounter in some members of your parish—and even in some priests—has nothing to do with your relationship with God. It would be foolish to let another's bad example deprive you of His gift of grace to you in the Mass.

17. **The Mass, with all its seriousness, seems so removed from everyday life. How does it affect me "here and now"?**

Actually, there is no better way to affect the "here and now" than by receiving the Maker of the Universe in the Eucharist at Mass.

The Mass allows us to be united with Jesus in the Eucharist. Through Holy Communion, we are nourished spiritually and grow in holiness. The Eucharist fortifies us in our quest to be saints and to live life to the full here and now. St. Thomas More (1478-1535) was one great example of this. He was an attorney, the key advisor to King Henry VIII of England, and the father of five. But he saw such value in the Mass that he went daily. A friend once asked him how he could afford to make time for Mass with all the things he had to do. His response was, "With all that I have to do, how can I not make time for Mass?" He likely had to call on the graces he received from daily Mass when he faced execution for "treason." His crime? Refusing to acknowledge Henry as the supreme authority of the Church of England rather than the pope.

Whether we are facing an exam, a big game, a business meeting, or an angry boss, we can find in the Mass the grace we need to be faithful to God's will for our lives, to be men and women of greatness in every circumstance. Grace gives us the strength we need to be diligent in our work, peaceful under pressure, clear-headed in conflicts, loving and pure in relationships, and humble in our interactions with others. The Mass helps us to keep our priorities straight so that we might truly achieve happiness in this life and in the next.

So nothing helps us to succeed more "here and now" than the Mass. Perhaps that is why people of faith have had the most positive impact on the world throughout history.

18. Why does Mass have to be so boring?

The late Kirk Cobain, lead singer of the popular '90s band Nirvana, once sang, "Here we are now. Entertain us!" This line is a good description of our modern youth culture. (Sadly, it must not have been a satisfying enough approach to life for Cobain. Despite having great fame and material wealth, he committed suicide at the age of twenty-seven.)

Seeking to be entertained all the time is not the key to happiness—nor is it the correct measure of judging the worth of something.

So the question "why is Mass so boring?" actually misses the point. The Mass is not supposed to entertain us but to sanctify us. If, by "boredom," you mean that Mass is not as exciting as listening to your iPod, instant messaging your friends, watching TV, or playing basketball, then a little "boredom" at Mass is to be expected.

When someone is seeking to build a relationship with another person, he or she is not primarily seeking to be entertained by him or her. What if you sat down at a nice restaurant and your date leaned over the table, looked you in the eye and said, "Entertain me! Make me laugh or something! You're starting to bore me!"? You would think he or she was a little unstable; you would get tired of them pretty quickly. Yet that is often the attitude we bring to our "date" with the Maker of the Universe at Mass.

Attending Mass is not about being entertained. It is about building our relationship with God; it is about listening to the Word of God in the Scriptures and encountering Jesus fully and personally in the Eucharist as we offer our lives to the Father in thanksgiving with Him.

So, to put it bluntly, don't go to Mass looking for entertainment. Entertainment is nothing next to what we can truly find at Mass. Go to Mass looking for God. You will likely find a host of important things in the process, like your very purpose for existing.

19. How can I "get into" Mass more?

Step One is understanding the Mass. You can have front row tickets to the Super Bowl, but if you do not know the rules of football you'll likely be focused on the foot-long sub sandwich more than the once-in-a-lifetime game. This simple book is designed to help you with Step One. We would also encourage you to check out the *Catechism*, paragraphs 1322–1419, or better yet, its entire second part, entitled "The Celebration of the Christian Mystery." It is beautiful, not overly long, and easy to understand.

Step Two in your quest to tap into the power of the Mass is to pursue a real, loving relationship with Jesus. We need to be in touch with Him throughout the week, not just for that one hour on Sunday. Think about it: How healthy would a marriage be if spouses just communed with each one hour each week (out of 168 total hours)? It wouldn't be healthy at all. If that is all the time we give to Jesus, Mass is going to seem like less of an encounter with the living

God and more like a burdensome collection of man-made rituals. Reflecting on this, Pope John Paul II once said that "Religion itself, without the wondrous discovery of the Son of God and communion with him who became our brother, becomes a mere set of principles which are increasingly difficult to understand, and rules which are increasingly hard to accept."[16] This book cannot really help you with Step Two. It is up to you to set aside time for daily prayer, Scripture study, regular confession, service to others, a yearly retreat, and fellowship.

In addition, here are some specific things you can do beforehand to prepare your mind and heart for Mass:

1. Check out the readings for the upcoming Sunday and meditate on them. They can be found online at www. usccb.org/nab. You could even start a small group to hang out, share a meal, and discuss how to apply the Sunday readings to your daily lives.

2. Arrive at Mass ten or even fifteen minutes early to quiet your heart in prayer. Better yet, if there is exposition and adoration of the Blessed Sacrament in your area, go! There is no substitute for adoring Jesus to get you ready to receive Him well.[17]

3. Above all, ask the Holy Spirit to help you more fully enter into the feast He has prepared for you.

4. Finally, during Mass, ask Mary to help you enter into prayer. She is "the model for each of us, called to receive the gift that Jesus makes of himself in the Eucharist."[18] If we can receive Jesus as she did, and offer ourselves to the Father with Him as she did, there is no doubt that we will also be filled with His presence and bring Him into the world as she did.

Chapter 2

THE HOLY EUCHARIST

20. **Was Jesus really speaking literally when He said,
"This is my body" about the Eucharist? That seems
too hard to believe.**

Take a look at the sixth chapter of John's gospel. Here,
Jesus is speaking to a large crowd who had been following
Him for a while, and He tells them—and us—something
extraordinary: that we must "eat His flesh" and "drink His
blood" to have "His life, eternal life," in us. He was so
explicit that He went on to repeat Himself several times
in several different ways (see Jn 6:48-58). Each instance in
this series of verses spells out, in the clearest possible terms,
that we must eat His flesh and drink His blood.

Many of the people who were following Jesus were naturally
shocked and appalled, and because of this teaching they
"returned to their former way of life and no longer followed
Him" (Jn 6:66). If the Savior of the world only meant these
sayings figuratively, wouldn't He have said to those people
(whom He was sent to save), "Don't be crazy! I didn't *really*
mean you have to eat and drink me. I just meant you have
to listen to my words, let them fill your hearts, and live
them out! You don't have to leave!"? But He didn't say
that. He let them go because He could not compromise on
this teaching. He then turned to His apostles, His closest

followers, and asked, "Do you want to leave me too?" (Jn 6:67). He was implying: "If so, then go ahead. Because I am not changing a word of what I just said—not even if you leave me as well and I am left with no one."

The response of Peter shows us what faith is all about: "Master, to whom shall we go? You have the words of eternal life" (Jn 6:68). In other words, "Jesus, I have no idea what you're talking about. I don't understand it. But I do believe in you. So I will accept anything you say. I trust in you." Faith is personal. It is not belief in one dogma or another—it is the acceptance of *every* dogma of faith because of our belief in a person, Jesus Christ.

Along with St. Peter, we have good reason to believe Jesus. He is the only person in history that substantiated everything He claimed with miracles that bore witness to His divinity—above all, the miracle of His resurrection.

So why would God insist that we receive Him physically? Because it did not satisfy His love for us to become human, teach us how to live, die on the Cross, and rise again for us. He wanted us to receive His love, not simply to hear about it. He wanted us to plug directly into His saving work for you on the Cross. In the words of St. Augustine, to "receive in this bread that which was hanged on the cross; [and] receive in this cup that which was poured from Christ's side."

Here is some additional information that might help you make sense of it all. You may recall that St. John the Baptist, when he first saw Jesus, said, "Behold, the Lamb of God who takes away the sin of the world" (Jn 1:29). Jesus was the perfect Lamb that would be slain to atone for sin. In the Old Testament, the Hebrew people used to offer animal sacrifices, including lambs, in atonement for sin. You may also remember that, on the night of the Passover, God's people were told to sprinkle the blood of a lamb on their doorposts. What you may not know is that these same people were told to eat the lamb (see Ex 12:8) that they had slain. Well, in the New Testament, we read about Jesus, the new Lamb, being crucified. Instead of doorposts, His blood would spilled on the wood of the Cross. In order to finish this sacrifice, though, you and I, His followers, need to "eat the Lamb." This is the Eucharist that you and I partake in at every Mass.

21. Are there any other New Testament passages that teach the Real Presence of Christ in the Eucharist?

Yes, there are. Among others ...

St. Paul talks about how the "Eucharist makes the Church" (CCC 1396) in 1 Corinthians 10:16-17:

> The cup of blessing that we bless, is it not a participation in the blood of Christ? The bread that we break, is it not a participation in the body of Christ? Because the loaf of bread is one, we, though many, are one body, for we all partake of the one loaf.

He speaks also in 1 Corinthians 11:23-30 about the importance of receiving Holy Communion worthily— specifically by recognizing the Real Presence of Jesus in the Eucharist and not just receiving Him as regular food:

> For I received from the Lord what I also handed on to you, that the Lord Jesus, on the night he was handed over, took bread, and, after he had given thanks, broke it and said, "This is my body that is for you. Do this in remembrance of me."
>
> In the same way also the cup, after supper, saying, "This cup is the new covenant in my blood. Do this,

as often as you drink it, in remembrance of me."
For as often as you eat this bread and drink the cup,
you proclaim the death of the Lord until he comes.

Therefore whoever eats the bread or drinks the
cup of the Lord unworthily will have to answer for
the body and blood of the Lord. A person should
examine himself, and so eat the bread and drink
the cup. For anyone who eats and drinks without
discerning the body, eats and drinks judgment on
himself. That is why many among you are ill and
infirm, and a considerable number are dying.

We see the early disciples recognizing the Risen Lord "in
the breaking of the bread" in Luke 24:13-35—after which
He instantly disappears, an indication of His presence now
with them in the Eucharist.

In Acts 2:41-43, we can see the centrality of the Mass in
the life of the early Church:

Those who accepted his message were baptized,
and about three thousand persons were added
that day. They devoted themselves to the teaching
of the apostles and to the communal life, to the
breaking of the bread and to the prayers. Awe came
upon everyone, and many wonders and signs were
done through the apostles.

Again, these are only some of the places, and this might
surprise you: the Mass is also described throughout the
book of Revelation (see question 90).

22. What evidence is there that the early Church believed in the Real Presence?

There is so much evidence of the early Church's faith in the
Real Presence of Jesus in the Eucharist that we could write a

whole book about it. Here we will just share a few quotations from Christians who were born before the year 200.

St. Paul (c. 10–c.67):

> The cup of blessing that we bless, is it not a participation in the blood of Christ? The bread that we break, is it not a participation in the body of Christ (1 Cor 10:16).
>
> Any one who eats and drinks without discerning the body eats and drinks judgment upon himself (1 Cor 1:29).

St. Ignatius of Antioch (c. 50–c. 117), a student of St. John the Apostle:

> I have no taste for the food that perishes nor for the pleasures of this life. I want the Bread of God which is the Flesh of Christ, who was the seed of David; and for drink I desire His blood which is love that cannot be destroyed (*Letter to the Romans*).

St. Justin Martyr (c. 100–165), a philosopher convert:

> So likewise have we been taught that the food which is blessed by the prayer of His word, and from which our blood and flesh ... are nourished, is the flesh and blood of that Jesus who was made flesh (*First Apology*).

St. Irenaeus (c. 130–202), who studied under St. Polycarp, a student of St. John the Apostle:

> For just as the bread which comes from the earth, having received the invocation of God, is no longer ordinary bread, but the Eucharist, consisting of two realities, earthly and heavenly, so our bodies, having received the Eucharist, are no longer corruptible,

because they have the hope of the resurrection (*Adversus Haereses*, "Against the Heresies").

Origen (185–254):

> When you have received the body of the Lord, you reverently exercise every care lest a particle of it fall and lest anything of the Consecrated Gift perish. You account yourselves guilty, and rightly do you so believe, if any of it be lost through negligence (*Homilies on Exodus*).

There are many other Church Fathers one could turn to for similar evidence of the early Church's belief in the Real Presence of Jesus in the Eucharist.

23. My Protestant friend says that the Church just invented the sacraments. Aren't they mentioned in the Bible?

The sacraments are not the inventions of man; they are gifts from Jesus Christ to His Church. Since He gave them to us, all seven sacraments can be found throughout the Bible. Here are just a few examples.

One of the many places we see <u>baptism</u> is in Matthew 28:19-20:

> Go, therefore, and make disciples of all nations, baptizing them in the name of the Father, and of the Son, and of the Holy Spirit, teaching them to observe all that I have commanded you.

The apostles (the first bishops) were confirming the baptized from the very beginning of the Church. Thus, we can see <u>confirmation</u> in Acts 8:14-17:

> Now when the apostles at Jerusalem heard that Samaria had received the word of God, they sent to

them Peter and John, who came down and prayed for them that they might receive the Holy Spirit; for it had not yet fallen on any of them, but they had only been baptized in the name of the Lord Jesus. Then they laid their hands on them and they received the Holy Spirit.

Jesus gave His apostles the <u>authority to forgive sins</u> in John 20:21-23:

Jesus said to them again, "Peace be with you. As the Father who sent me, even so I send you." And when He had said this, He breathed on them, and said to them, "Receive the Holy Spirit. If you forgive the sins of any, they are forgiven. If you retain the sins of any, they are retained."

The <u>anointing of the sick</u> is very explicitly described in James 5:14-15:

Is any among you sick? Let him call for the presbyters of the Church, and let them pray over him, anointing him with oil in the name of the Lord; and the prayer of faith will save the sick man, and the Lord will raise him up; and if he has committed sins, he will be forgiven.

The grace-filled sacrament of <u>marriage</u> is beautifully described by St. Paul in Ephesians 5:25; 32:

Husbands, love your wives, even as Christ loved the Church ... This is a great mystery (*sacramentum*), but I speak in reference to Christ and the Church.

Acts 1:21-26 describes how Matthias was chosen and ordained to be an apostle—a bishop set apart to serve the Church by his sacramental ministry. This is one of the passages in which we see the sacrament of <u>holy orders</u> conferred.

To see where the <u>Eucharist</u> (and the Mass) is in the Bible, check out questions 21, 22, 53, and 90.

Again, these are just a few examples of evidence for the sacraments in the New Testament.

24. Isn't eating the body and blood of Jesus cannibalism?

No, it is not. Cannibalism is eating the flesh of a dead human being. Jesus Christ in the Eucharist is fully alive. After we receive Him, His *Real Presence* remains alive and well within us (for as long as the appearance of the bread and wine remains). If we were to liken our reception of Jesus in Holy Communion to anything else in our earthly lives, it would be most like the one-flesh union of a married couple. The living God unites Himself to us physically and fills us with His own divine life so that we may be spiritually fruitful. The love that God has for us is often likened to the love of a husband for his wife (see Ephesians, chapter five). The Eucharist is the consummation of that covenant love between God and His people. That is how close our God wants to be with us and how deeply He loves us … a far cry from the barbaric practice of cannibalism!

If you really think about it, when we receive communion it is more like God consuming us than our consuming God. If you eat a donut it becomes part of you because you are bigger than that donut. God is greater than you, so that if you receive God, you become part of Him.[19]

25. At what point during the Mass are the bread and wine changed into the body and blood of Christ?

During the Eucharist Prayer, the priest prays the words of consecration. At this point, the bread and wine are "transubstantiated" and become the sacred body and blood of Jesus. This is when the priest solemnly pronounces the words of Christ: "This is my body" and "This is my blood," elevating the host and the chalice immediately afterward. Notice that the priest doesn't say "This is the body of Jesus," but rather, "This is *my* body." This is because the priest, during the Mass, is acting *in persona Christi* ("in the person of Christ"); he literally is standing in for Jesus when celebrating the Eucharist.[20] (See CCC 1377 and 1413 for more on this topic.)

26. **After the bread and wine at Mass are changed into the body and blood of Christ, would a DNA test on them show human flesh and blood?**

No. At the Last Supper when Jesus said "This is my body," the host that He held in His hands continued to have the physical properties of bread: it still looked, felt, and tasted like unleavened bread. Yet the apostles took Jesus at His word. It was no longer bread, it was Jesus himself, and this miraculous change has occurred at every valid Mass since then. So if the bread does not change in appearance, then how *does* it change? It changes in *substance*. Thus, we call this change *transubstantiation*.

In philosophical language, substance refers to the "whatness" of something. A grain of wheat changes in size, shape, and color as it sprouts and grows, but it remains an individual plant of its species: its properties (the "appearances") change, while its substance ("what it is") stays the same.

Miraculously, the opposite occurs in the consecration of the Eucharist. Even though the physical properties of bread and wine are still there, the underlying substance

"bread" changes into the substance "body and blood of
Christ." After the consecration, the host is no longer a
piece of bread; it is Jesus. It is not Jesus *present* somehow
"in" bread; it is Jesus really present *under the appearance*
(i.e., form) of bread. It is 100 percent Jesus—His body,
blood, soul, and divinity.

27. **Sometimes my parish offers communicants the cup
     as well as the host. Does the consecration remove the
     possibility of being infected with another's germs?**

No. Although the bread and wine offered at Mass is
changed *in substance* from bread and wine into Jesus,
the *appearance* (and chemical properties) of bread and
wine remain. These observable aspects of the bread
and wine are referred to in philosophical language as
accidents. ("Accident," in this context, does not mean "an
unintentional mistake.") Whereas substance refers to the
"what-ness" of a thing, accidents are not the thing itself, but
various quantitative and qualitative aspects of the thing.
For example, a particular dog is white, has four legs, coarse
hair, and very large teeth. "Dog" is the substance—"what"
it is; "white, quadruped, coarse-haired, and large-toothed"
are the accidents. If that dog got hit by a car and was left
hairless, toothless, and with only two legs, it does not
become some other kind of "freak" animal. It remains a
dog. The substance remains the same, even if the accidents
change. At Mass, a miracle happens that is seen nowhere
else on earth: the substance changes while the accidents
remain the same.

Because the accidents of the wine remain, it can still
conduct and transmit germs from one person to the next
the same way that unconsecrated wine can—though the
alcohol in the wine (which is an accident that remains)

and the silver of the cup do help to stop the transmission of germs somewhat.

28. **On most Sundays at my parish only consecrated hosts are distributed at communion. Shouldn't we receive both the body and the blood of Christ at every Mass?**

While we can refer separately to Jesus' "sacred body" and "precious blood," after the consecration Jesus is truly present—body, blood, soul, and divinity—both in the host and in the cup.

If you only receive the host, you have received Jesus. If you only receive from the cup, you have received Jesus. Because of this, it is not necessary to receive both the host and the cup. However, sometimes both forms are distributed at communion because this more fully *symbolizes* what Jesus accomplished on the Cross when His body and blood were separated for us. This separation is a sign of His death. It also recalls His victory over death by His rising and ascending into heaven, reminding us that the One whom we receive is alive and glorified.

29. **Is the Real Presence of Christ in the Eucharist something that we just have to accept on faith, then?**

The words of One who died and rose again should be enough "proof" for us. Yet Jesus Christ, the Good Teacher, gradually prepared His disciples for the great mystery that He would reveal in the Blessed Sacrament. The discourse on the Eucharist in chapter six of John's gospel immediately follows a miraculous multiplication of loaves and fish to feed a hungry crowd. Jesus showed His followers that He could feed them, at will, with earthly food, then He told them that one day He would feed them with heavenly food—His own body and blood.

That being said, there have been many miracles since the time of Christ that attest to the Real Presence of Jesus in the Eucharist. If you do a Google search of the words "miracles of the Eucharist," you will find many examples.

Here's one: In Lanciano, Italy, in the eighth century, a priest was celebrating Mass and started to wonder whether the consecrated host in his hands truly was the body of Christ. As these thoughts crossed his mind, the host took on the appearance of human flesh and began to bleed, with the blood dripping on the altar. That host is preserved to this day in a monstrance in Lanciano.

In the 1980s, a scientist who was a professed atheist requested permission to study the Lanciano event, hoping to disprove the miracle. His investigation determined that, even though the preserved host is dried out after more than a thousand years, it is still fresh. Scientific testing proved that it is actually human heart tissue, with a blood type of "AB positive." Every part of a heart that is required to function was present in the host. As a result of these findings, the scientist became a Catholic. If you visit Lanciano today, you can see the results of his study posted on the wall of the parish church. The study is entitled, "And the Word was Made Flesh."

Remember: Jesus is not some fictional character in an historical novel. Nor is He far away in some distant heaven, leaving us alone down here to do the best we can. He is alive and well and present to us in the Eucharist, offering us eternal life and love. This love is too great for us to remain indifferent to it—or to relegate it to an hour a week. The Son of God offers His whole heart and life to us. He wants nothing less in return. Jesus gives us His perfect heart and wants our imperfect hearts in exchange, just as they are (though He loves far us too much to let them stay that way!).[21]

30. Doesn't the Eucharist split Jesus' body into millions of pieces?

No. In the Eucharist, we are talking about Christ being physically present in a *sacramental* way. God is infinite, while we are finite. He can give His whole self, living and undivided, to one person and still have His whole self to give to the next person in line. In this we know the extent of His love for us: that our God, who exists outside of space and time, gives us His Son, whole and entire, every time we receive the Holy Eucharist.

God created us in His image and likeness (see Gn 1:27), and so an analogy from human experience might be helpful here. We can observe a reflection of God's "infiniteness" in our own hearts when we love. For example, both authors of this book are the fathers of several children. We can testify that it is possible to love each of our kids with our whole heart.

31. I don't feel any holier after I receive communion. Is that normal?

The movement of God's grace in our souls is not necessarily accompanied by emotional responses, immediately noticeable interior conversion or deep insights. And it is rare for the movement of God's grace to be perceived by the physical senses. (In fact, this would be an extraordinary phenomenon that should be discussed with a priest or spiritual director to test its legitimacy.)

When God does work in our souls in a way that is noticeable to us, this is a gift called *consolation*, a fitting word since it is such a wonderful experience. For instance, we might feel great peace or joy after receiving communion, our hearts may overflow with the love of God, or something that was deeply troubling us may become instantly clear, bringing us a deep sense of calm. Besides bringing consolations from God, Mass may also make us feel different simply because we respond emotionally to our knowledge of what we have just received, but this can also be considered a grace.

Such experiences and feelings come and go. This is especially true with regard to emotions. Our emotions are not fully under the control of our intellects. A husband might know the beauty of his wife and the great gift she is to him. Over the course of a long marriage, this knowledge sometimes leads to intense emotion while at other times it does not.

Just as it would be extremely short-sighted to seek a marriage built primarily on emotional feelings and fun experiences, it is dangerous to base our relationship with God on how it "feels" in the moment. We doubt that St. Peter "felt good" when he was dying, hung upside down on a cross. Yet, at that moment, he was following Christ in the closest and most profound way possible. Many saints experienced intense spiritual "dryness." Some knew this desolate condition for many years. They felt nothing at all when they were praying. Was something wrong with them? No.

God might let us experience dryness for one of two reasons: Either there is something He wants us to change (perhaps a complacent relationship with Him), or we're right on target and He wants to test our love for Him. It's

easy to love God when it "feels good." But God wants to
be more than our spiritual drug, there to give us a "God
high." He wants us to love Him, even when we do not feel
such love emotionally. (Love is not a feeling but a choice.)
Consolation is a little gift, a reminder of God's love for us,
which He *sometimes* gives us when we need it. Pressing on
in our devotion when we feel nothing is a sign of our love
for Him.

**32. A friend of my mother said that we should receive
communion only on the tongue. Is that correct?**

No. Your mother's friend is trying to make a personal
preference the universal law of the Church. It is true,
however, that communion in the hand has been a practice
in the United States only since 1977. Prior to that,
Catholics in this country (and indeed around the world)
were required to receive on the tongue. On June 17, 1977,
the bishops of the United States, following a permission
given them by Rome, allowed us to receive communion in
the hand as an option.[22]

So, while there are some countries in which you can receive
only on the tongue, the *General Instruction of the Roman
Missal* (GIRM), the official "rule book" describing the
rituals of the Mass, states that a person can receive either
on the tongue or in the hand: "The consecrated host may
be received either on the tongue or in the hand, at the
discretion of each communicant."[23]

Some may prefer to receive on the tongue because they
perceive it to be more reverent, because there is less chance
of dropping the host, because they do not want to have
crumbs on their hands after receiving, or because they
would prefer that fewer people handle the host. Others

may prefer to receive in the hand out of the fear of germs or because some extraordinary ministers are awkward in distributing communion on the tongue. There could be many reasons, both spiritual and practical, for either preference. Whatever the reason your mother's friend has for preferring to receive on his tongue, it would be wrong for him to require more of you than the Church does. On the other hand, it would also be wrong for anyone, even a priest, to make a communicant who prefers to receive the Eucharist on the tongue feel awkward about his or her preference.

33. Does the Eucharist have any impact on society?

Faith fuels people. It is what makes them "tick." And people form societies and change the world. So how has faith, specifically in the Eucharist, fueled people to impact society?

Our Western civilization, full of beautiful ideals, from freedom and democracy to care for the poor, is founded on core beliefs about our God-given human dignity. (This is echoed in the eloquent words of Thomas Jefferson in the *Declaration of Independence*, "We hold these truths to be self-evident, that all men are created equal.") The beliefs arose, not by accident, out of a profoundly Christian world. Catholicism awakened the world to the concept of human dignity more than any other philosophy or belief system had ever done. That the Son of God would give His life for us, and allow every person to receive Him physically in the Eucharist—rich and poor, sick and well, young and old—reveals who we are in the eyes of God. A man is not worth how much money he has in the bank; he is "worth" God the Son to God the Father. He is worth the Eucharist.

The Church has reflected on these things for millennia. This is what fueled the Catholic Church to civilize many of the lands that our ancestors came from, starting (literally inventing) universities, hospitals, countless social programs to serve the poor, protecting classical learning in the midst of barbarian invaders, and commissioning most of the art that you see today in Europe. It was probably a Catholic missionary who taught your great-great-great-great-grandfather, "Thor, it isn't OK to club your wife because you had a bad day at work!"

Believing that God calls us to progress even to the point of becoming like Him has also inspired countless Christians throughout history to apply this principle to the temporal world (which, by the way, they saw as good because God entered it when His Son became flesh) and to excel in science and technology. (Did you know a nineteenth-century Augustinian monk, Fr. Gregor Mendel, is considered the father of genetics?)

This simple concept of human dignity is still at the basis of the Catholic Church's social teachings as she continues to encourage human development and to fight "barbarism" in its many forms today. Every Church teaching, from the Gospel of Life to our obligation to help the poor and support the rights of workers, can be summed up in this: Do not diminish man's God-given worth. The love shown to us in the Eucharist continues to fuel the Church in her fight for a more humane world—a society founded on the principle of human dignity.

Chapter 3

GOD'S TIME

34. Why does the Church have its own calendar?

The Church calendar, also called the "liturgical year," is the yearly cycle of seasons and days by which we celebrate various events in the life of Christ and what He has done for us. These celebrations are primarily observed in the prayers of the liturgy.

While the "theme" of every Mass is the *Paschal Mystery*—Jesus' dying, rising, and ascending into heaven during the Passover season—we celebrate other aspects of Christ's life at Mass throughout the liturgical year (e.g., the Annunciation when He was conceived, or Christmas when He was born) because they help us "unpack" the Paschal Mystery in all its fullness (see CCC 1171). We also get a fuller understanding of the effects of the Paschal Mystery in our lives and how we are to respond to it by honoring the martyrs and saints, especially Mary (who responded perfectly to Christ's redemptive work and whose life is commemorated on several days in the Church calendar).

This cycle of liturgical celebrations sanctifies the passage of time. We Catholics believe that just about everything—including time—can be made holy. God is greater than time. When Jesus, the eternal Son of God entered time by becoming flesh, time itself was made sacred. The liturgical year is a reminder of this reality. Our days and seasons, like our lives, are now tied to the life of Jesus Christ—year after year. By observing special liturgical days in the course of our everyday lives, we incorporate into them the very things that will bring us closer to Jesus.

The Church calendar is also a reminder to hope. Though time moves us ever closer to death, the constant celebration of the death and resurrection of Christ, which "permeates with its powerful energy our old time" (CCC 1169), is a constant reminder that we are also moving toward heaven and toward the end of time, when Jesus will subject all things to Himself, even death (see 1 Cor 15:25-26 and 55).

35. What are the liturgical seasons?

The liturgical year of the Church consists of five seasons:

- *Advent* begins the liturgical year. This season starts on the fourth Sunday before Christmas. During Advent, we remember God's promises to His chosen people, by which He prepared the world for the coming of Christ. During this time, we prepare to welcome Him at Christmas and when He comes again. Through our penances and self-denial we learn to recognize and receive Him in the many ways in which He comes to us every day.

- *Christmas*, of course, is the celebration of the birth of Christ. The Christmas season begins with the Solemnity of Christmas, which starts on the vigil of December 25th (Christmas Eve). It includes the Solemnity of the Mother of God (New Year's Day), the Epiphany (when the Magi came to worship Jesus), and concludes with the celebration of the baptism of the Lord in early January.

- *Lent* is a season of forty days leading up to Easter. During Lent we prepare our hearts for the celebration of the passion, death, and resurrection of Jesus. The forty days symbolize the forty years that the Israelites spent in the desert before entering the Promised Land, and the forty days that Jesus spent in the desert fasting and praying before beginning His public ministry. During Lent, we follow Jesus into the desert of our hearts, focusing more intensely on our interior life, making sacrifices as penance and to overcome spiritual distractions, and setting aside more time for prayer and service to others. During the Lenten season, Catholics are required to abstain from meat on Fridays and to fast and abstain from meat on Ash Wednesday and Good Friday (see *Code of Canon Law*, 1249–1251). Lent concludes with the Triduum, a three-day period from Holy Thursday to Holy Saturday, commemorating the Last Supper and the Passion and death of Our Lord.

- *Easter* is the season that celebrates the resurrection of Jesus Christ. It begins on the night Jesus rose from the dead, the Saturday night (vigil) before Easter Sunday, with the Easter Vigil Mass, which is the most elaborate and solemn Mass of the liturgical year. The Solemnity of Easter is celebrated with its "octave," that is, for a total of eight days, including the Second Sunday of Easter. One week after the Seventh Sunday of Easter, the Easter season ends on the evening of Pentecost Sunday, when we celebrate the descent of the Holy Spirit on the apostles.

- *Ordinary Time* is the period of time between the Christmas and Lenten seasons, and then between the

Easter and Advent seasons. It is the longest liturgical season and is not marked by any particular holy day. But this is not why it is called "ordinary." It takes its name from the Latin *ordo*, meaning "order," referring to the ordered days of the Church calendar. During ordinary time we focus on walking and growing with the Lord in our everyday life.

36. **Aren't some Christian holy days, such as Christmas, just pagan holidays that were "Christianized"?**

Yes. Christianity assimilates what is human and redeems it, baptizes it, fulfills it, and raises it to new dignity. That is what Jesus did when He became flesh, what the Holy Spirit did when He inspired men to record the Word of God in human words and literary genres, and that is what God did for us when we were baptized and made His children. That is also what the Catholic Church did when determining the dates to commemorate and celebrate specific events and mysteries of our faith. It baptized "time" itself, making both natural time and pagan time become, in a sense, Christian time.

Christmas is an excellent example of this. Although we do not know for sure the exact day Jesus was born, many historians believe it was around the date of December 25. The Church chose to replace the pagan celebration of Winter Solstice (the shortest day of the year which was marked by many rituals to celebrate the return of light) with the celebration of the birth of God. This shows us some of the wisdom of the early Church. You do not take something bad away and leave a void. Rather, you fill it with something good. It is fitting to celebrate the coming into our world of the "the light [that] shines in the darkness" (Jn 1:5) on the day when the sunlight hours begin to lengthen. Six months earlier, we celebrate the birth of John the Baptist on June 24, the Summer Solstice. St. John the Baptist signifies all the prophets of the Old Testament pointing the way to Jesus. He once said "He must increase, but I must decrease" (Jn 3:30). Appropriately, from the day chosen to celebrate his birth the days get shorter and shorter until we reach Christmas. Another example is Lent. "Lent" comes from the Ango-Saxon word *Lethen*, which simply means "Spring." Lent coincides with the start of spring. This is an appropriate title for this season, since a season of penance is also a season of spiritual re-birth.

It was not only Old Testament prophecy that pointed to Christ, but many of the dreams and longings of the human heart that are expressed in religions and myths throughout history. Even the cosmos, the seasons and the elements of the natural world point to God and His action in our lives. The Liturgy assimilates and baptizes all of this, fulfilling what is human in what is divine, and what is natural in the supernatural.

And when the Church celebrates these great holy days (a.k.a. "holidays") on earth, we can count on the fact that we are celebrating them together with the Church in heaven (see Mt 16:19).

37. **Why do priests wear different colored vestments during the various liturgical seasons?**

Just as the red of Valentine's Day and the orange of Halloween (All Hallows' Eve) symbolically suggest what those days celebrate, so too the liturgical seasons and specific days on the Church calendar have colors associated with them to help us enter into the sacred celebration.

These colors are worn by the priest and are often used to adorn the Church as well.

- *White* symbolizes joy, purity, and light, and is used during the Easter and Christmas seasons and on special days commemorating our Lord and His saints. It is also used on festive occasions like baptisms and weddings, and often at funerals as a reminder of the resurrection of Jesus and thus a reminder to hope for our loved ones who will be raised to eternal life at the end of time. (Violet and black can also be worn for funerals, though black is used less commonly now than in the past.)

- *Red* symbolizes blood and fire, and is used on Palm Sunday and Good Friday (both of which focus on Jesus' crucifixion), days commemorating martyrs, on Pentecost Sunday (the day the Holy Spirit descended on Mary and the apostles), and on feasts of the apostles and evangelists.

- *Green* symbolizes hope, peace, and growth. It is used during the season of Ordinary Time.

- *Violet (or purple)* signifies both penance and royalty. It is used in the penitential seasons of Advent and Lent. On the third Sunday of Advent ("*Gaudete* Sunday") and the fourth Sunday of Lent ("*Laetare* Sunday"), rose-colored vestments are traditionally worn instead of purple to symbolize the joy we should feel that the end of these penitential seasons is near. (Both *Gaudete* and *Laetare* can be translated "rejoice").

These specified colors can vary from place to place but rarely do. For example, many Asian cultures see white as a color of mourning, so certain regions might have permission from the Vatican to use a more fitting color for them on high feast days. Also, on more solemn days, a priest has permission to use his best, most festive vestments if they are not of the appointed color. Gold can also be used on very special liturgical celebrations in certain countries, including the United States, as a replacement for white, red, or green (but not violet or black). Silver may also be used in place of white.

38. Does the Church consider some Holy Days or feasts more important than others?

Yes. Just as your wedding anniversary is more important to you than the first Monday of December (provided that Monday isn't your birthday!), so the Church considers certain days more important than others and celebrates them with greater solemnity.

The Church has decreed that Christmas and Easter are the pre-eminent holy days because they highlight the dramatic realities of the birth and resurrection of Jesus. Depending on what is being celebrated, days in the Church calendar vary in importance, from memorials (usually commemorating a saint), through feast days, to solemnities, which are the highest holy days. The level of a celebration may vary from place to place: for instance, St. Patrick's Day is a solemnity in Ireland but a memorial elsewhere.

All of the days on the church calendar except certain solemnities and Feasts of the Lord, which commemorate various aspects of Jesus' life, are trumped by Sunday, which is a category all its own. Each Sunday is like a mini-Easter, celebrating the resurrection. If one of these solemnities or feasts falls on a Sunday the readings pertaining to that day are used rather than those of the given Sunday.

39.   What is the Triduum?

The *Triduum* (literally, "three days") is the liturgical celebration of the suffering (or "passion"), death, and resurrection of Jesus Christ. It begins with the evening of Holy Thursday, when Jesus instituted the Holy Eucharist, ordained the first priests, and entered into His agony in the Garden of Gethsemane through His crucifixion, death, and burial on Good Friday, to the Easter Vigil on Holy Saturday. It follows the Jewish tradition of counting days from sundown. Since every Mass is the re-presentation of the Paschal Mystery (i.e., the death, resurrection, and ascension of Christ), the Triduum, celebrating the days when His dying and rising actually happened, marks the highpoint of the Church's liturgical year.

The Triduum should be seen as a single liturgical celebration spanning three days rather than three separate celebrations. This reality is expressed in the following ways: the Mass of the Lord's Supper on Holy Thursday evening has no final blessing, the service (not a Mass) on Good Friday afternoon has no opening prayer or final blessing, and the Easter Vigil Mass on Holy Saturday has no opening prayer as in other Masses.

Christ's dying and rising are inseparable. The power of His resurrection is already present in the crucifixion, transforming the very meaning of death for all of us. This is why His final words on the Cross were "it is finished" (Jn 19:30): He had already won the victory over sin and death. This is also why the gospel of Matthew tells us many saints rose from their graves right when He died (see Mt 27:52-53). Thus, we refer to "Good Friday." Because of the resurrection, Christ's death is our ultimate victory. If He had not died He could not have conquered sin and death for us. By the one act of His dying and rising He redeemed the world so that we may be made one with Him.

40. What are holy days of obligation?

Holy days of obligation are days on which "the faithful are obliged to participate in the Mass. Moreover, they are to abstain from those works and affairs which hinder the worship to be rendered to God, the joy proper to the Lord's day, or the suitable relaxation of mind and body" (*Code of Canon Law*, 1247). In other words, a holy day of obligation belongs primarily to God. Participating in the worship of the Mass on such holy days is foundational to the Christian life (see CCC 2181).

Ever since the first days of the Church, every Sunday has been celebrated as a holy day of obligation. Certain feast days and solemnities, which vary according to national customs, are also observed as holy days of obligation, including Christmas (December 25), the Epiphany (celebrated in the United States on the Sunday following January 1), the Ascension of Christ (varies), the feast of the body and blood of Christ/Corpus Christi (celebrated in the United States on the second Sunday after Pentecost), the Solemnity of Mary the Mother of God (January 1), her Immaculate Conception (December 8), her Assumption (August 15), the feast of Saint Joseph (March 19), the feast of Saints Peter and Paul (June 29), and the feast of All Saints (November 1). (See *Code of Canon Law*, 1246; quoted in CCC 2177.)

The bishops (i.e., the episcopal conference) in a given country or region may determine which specific holy days of obligation will be observed in their territory. They may also transfer the observance of a particular feast to the nearest Sunday (see *Code*, 1246:2). In the United States, for example, the feasts of St. Joseph and of Sts. Peter and Paul are not holy days of obligation. In addition, since January 1, 1993, Mass attendance on the solemnities of the Mother of God (January 1), All Saints (November 1), and the Assumption of Mary (August 15) is not required if these feasts fall on a Saturday or Monday. Also, the states of the western U.S. have been given permission to transfer observance of the Ascension from the sixth Thursday after Easter to the following Sunday.

Listen to the Sunday Mass announcements and check out your parish bulletin for information about upcoming holy days of obligation.

41.   Do I really have to go to Mass every Sunday?

Yes, you do. Every Sunday is a holy day of obligation. God commands us to "keep holy the Sabbath" (see the third commandment), and the Church has taught since the beginning that, at minimum, we are to fulfill this commandment by going to Mass every Sunday. (Note: The Sunday Vigil Mass on Saturday evening also fulfills our "Sunday obligation" to God. According to the Church's calendar, Sunday actually begins on Saturday evening.)

On Sunday, nothing should come in the way of worship, service and relaxation (CCC 2185). We know this can be tough at times. There are many demands and opportunities that come up on Sunday that can conflict with Mass. But just ask yourself, "If my favorite band was at the Church tonight, would I get there?", or, "If there was a bag of money for me on the altar, would I go to get it?" If you would make it for that and not the Eucharist, what does that say about where God fits in your list of priorities?

In addition, God desires to share with us something far greater than merely material possessions. He gives us His very self in the Eucharist! What treasure on earth could ever compare?

42. So why does God take Sunday so seriously?

Because He takes our freedom so seriously. The third commandment, like all the others, was not given to us to bind us to yet another religious obligation but to set us free. Although we may not see it immediately, following the laws of God actually "frees" us—liberates us. Here's how this is so with the third commandment.

God originally commanded His people, Israel, to rest and worship on the Sabbath day as a sign that they did not belong to a Pharaoh (the earthly ruler) but to Him. They were meant for more than just "working for Pharaoh."

They did not exist for servile work but for God! The same holds true today: By honoring God's commandment to worship Him at least one day per week (in the manner He established—the Eucharistic celebration known as "Mass"), it declares our freedom. It reminds us that we aren't slaves to our work, and that "work is for the man and not man for work."[24] We show the world—and remind ourselves—that we do not ultimately live for this world, but for God, and that our number one priority is beyond this world and in the heavenly promised land to come.

43. Why do we go on Sunday versus another day of the week?

In most places, Mass is available to Catholics every day of the week but is mandated on Sunday, which is why most Catholics only go to Mass on that day.

God commanded His people to set aside the Sabbath for rest and prayer (see the third commandment). This is modeled on God's own "rest" following the six days of Creation. Genesis tells us that on the seventh day, after God had created everything, He "rested" (see Gn 2:1-3).

The people of God before Christ came, and Jews to this day, observe the Sabbath rest on Saturday, the seventh and final day of the week. Christians have always observed the third commandment by keeping Sunday, rather than Saturday, holy. So, you might ask, why do we worship on Sunday? Sunday, which is regarded as the first day of the week, is the day that God began His work of creation. Jesus rose from the dead on a Sunday. Therefore, Christians have always regarded it as the first day of the "new creation"—inaugurated by the resurrection and the new holy day.[25]

Sunday is also figuratively referred to as the "eighth day"—the day that follows the completion of the old creation (which Genesis describes as occurring in seven days) and inaugurates a new (supernatural) creation that awaits us just beyond the seven-day cycle of time—the "day" of eternity. It is because of this that many baptismal fonts are eight sided. At that font we enter into this new creation. As St. Paul put it, "If anyone is in Christ he is a new creation. The old is passed away; now all is new!" (2 Cor 5:17).

Sunday worship is not a discontinuation of the Sabbath observed before Christ on Saturday, but rather, is one of many ways in which the Old Covenant (i.e., Testament) has been fulfilled and completed in Christ.

44. **Will it really affect my relationship with God if I miss Mass on a Sunday or holy day of obligation?**

For a Catholic to skip Mass deliberately on a holy day of obligation (i.e., you could have gone but chose not to) is a grave sin (CCC 2181). In the case of Sunday Mass, it is also a breaking of the third commandment to "Keep holy the Sabbath" (Ex 20:8). When we commit a grave or serious sin with full knowledge and full freedom we are in mortal sin and no longer are in the "state of grace."

What does all this mean? Well, in baptism, we are admitted into an intimate relationship with God, receiving His very inner life, His grace. When we deliberately commit grave sin, we rupture this relationship with God—choosing our will over His divine will. Some sins are small and weaken rather than break off the relationship. We call these "venial" sins. Others are very serious. We call these "mortal" (which means "deadly"; see 1 Jn 5:16-17) sins. Ignoring a clear commandment of God—for instance, by intentionally missing Mass—would be considered a mortal sin, if done with sufficient freedom and knowledge. If someone knows about this commandment, understands its importance, and then simply ignores it, can that person really say he or she loves God? After all, love is proven through our actions more than our words. (It is important to note that there are times when someone cannot get to Mass. For example, if you are sick, do not have a ride, or your job demands that you work from Saturday evening through Sunday evening, such as a doctor or nurse on call. It is obviously not a sin to miss Mass under such circumstances, since a deliberate act of the will is necessary for any act to be sinful.)

All sins aside, when you miss Mass you miss out on the richest encounter you can have with God on earth. You miss the grace that comes with the Eucharist and from hearing the Word of God preached. You also miss the benefits of fellowship with the wider community of Catholic believers.

45. What if I have deliberately skipped Mass on a Sunday or holy day of obligation? What should I do?

If you deliberately miss Mass on a day when the Church requires you to attend, simply repent of this sin, trust in the mercy of God, and make plans to go to confession before you again receive Jesus in the Eucharist. (You should still go to Mass on the next Sunday or holy day, even if you have not yet gone to confession and so are not are not properly disposed to receive). Never lose hope. God is always ready to receive us if we simply turn back to Him.

Whenever we have, objectively-speaking, committed a mortal sin, it is helpful to remember the words of St. Augustine: "Two criminals were crucified with Christ. One was saved; do not despair. One was not; do not presume."

"Do not despair." Jesus wants to commune with us here on earth and in heaven—so much so that He actually laid down His very life to give us this wondrous gift. Remember the story of the Prodigal Son (see Lk 14:11-32)? One of the morals of this parable is that mortal sin is not God rejecting us, but our rejecting Him. Yet, just like the son in the parable, when we turn back to God, we will find our forgiving Father running out to meet us.

While we absolutely should not despair, we should also not presume on God's mercy, either. It is easy for us to forget that sinning against a loving God is a serious issue. In recent decades, some in the Church have over-emphasized God's love and mercy to the exclusion of His justice. It seems that many people today think sin—especially the sin of skipping Mass—is no big deal. As Pope Benedict points out, we are "surrounded by a culture that tends to eliminate the sense of sin ...[but, the] loss of a consciousness of sin always entails a certain superficiality in the understanding of God's love,"[26] which was revealed to us fully in Christ's death for our sins. God, who created and redeemed us, deserves our love, and His laws demand our adherence. It is crucial to remember that there can be eternal consequences for our actions if we do not repent of them. (Remember—Jesus did not die for nothing; our souls were at stake.) If we die in a state of mortal sin, having rejected God's laws and refusing to repent, we will be excluded from communion with Him in eternity—by our own choosing.

The sacrament of reconciliation is the ordinary and sure way to fix things when we commit a serious sin. Why? Because God set it up that way. In John 20:20-23, Jesus gave to His apostles, the Church's first bishops, the authority to forgive sins. Some might say, "why not just go straight to God to repent?" We cannot adequately judge our own souls or our spiritual state before God. We cannot be certain whether we had full knowledge or freedom when we committed a particular sin, both of which are necessary for an objectively "grave" sin to be a subjectively mortal sin. (We may not even know whether the sin involved objectively grave matter.) Also, we cannot judge whether we have repented with perfect contrition (i.e., repentance solely out of our love for God), which is necessary for the restoration of sanctifying grace apart from the sacrament of reconciliation. Even St. Paul said that he did not judge himself (see 1 Cor 4:3). When we encounter Jesus in the confession, though, and hear the words of absolution spoken by His priest—"I absolve you from your sins, in the name of the Father, and of the Son, and of the Holy Spirit"—we do not have to wonder about the state of our souls. We have been made clean; we have been restored to God's grace and reconciled with His Church (see CCC 1496).

Find the happy middle road between guilt and trust, fear and confidence. Make sure you take your sins seriously, but make sure that you also take seriously the mercy of God and your dignity as His son or daughter which no sin, however grave, can take away.

46. How can the Church make missing Mass such a serious sin?

The Church did not arbitrarily determine how serious a sin it is to miss Sunday Mass, nor did she invent confession and its necessity—God did. The Church is simply presenting these truths, clarifying them for us, and acting accordingly in her pastoral care for souls. The Church can do this because Jesus gave it His authority—and along with it, the promise of the Holy Spirit's guidance when it teaches on faith and morals (see Mt 16:19, 18:18, 28:20; CCC 553, 874, among others).

Here is an analogy that may help you understand why Jesus established His teaching and governing authority in a visible Church here on earth.

In 1787, the Founding Fathers of the United States did not simply draw up the Constitution and send a message out to the entire country to "go and figure out what the Constitution means for yourself—and decide for yourself when you are breaking the law." Such a move would have led to disorder, even chaos. Instead, in the same Constitution, they established a Supreme Court to have the final say in interpreting and applying disputed laws. Without this kind of authority structure in place, America would not have lasted very long as a nation.

In a similar (though infinitely more profound) way, Jesus did not just leave us a Book of His laws. Rather, He left us an organized Church with the authority to apply His teachings, including those in the Book (i.e., the Bible), to the lives of His followers. He set aside twelve apostles to lead the Church (see Jn 15:16, 20:21, Lk 22:29-30) and placed St. Peter, the first Bishop of Rome, as their head, giving him the "keys" of the kingdom (Mt 16:19). (In the Bible, *keys* = ultimate delegated authority; see Is 22:22.)

As the Church grew, the apostles appointed bishops to replace them, who likewise appointed successors, continuing down to the bishops of today. St. Peter's God-given authority as the Vicar of Christ has been passed down to Pope Benedict XVI, the 265th bishop of Rome.

The doctrinal authority of the Church (exercised by the bishops united with the pope or by the pope teaching alone) is known as the *Magisterium*, which safeguards the deposit of faith found in Sacred Scripture and Sacred Tradition (see CCC 86, 95, 100). Without the Magisterium in place, the Church would not have lasted very long. It would have split into major factions (or even new types of "churches") every time a major theological conflict arose.

Just as the U.S. Supreme Court gives us a final word when interpreting the Constitution, the Magisterium has the final word in interpreting matters of faith and morals. Unlike the Supreme Court, though, the Magisterium has a divine guarantee that it will be preserved from error when it teaches about faith and morals (see Mt 16:16-19; Jn 14:25-26; CCC 890-891).

In light of the earliest traditions in Christian worship, the Magisterium has always taught that Sunday Mass is essential for Christian life and necessary for the fulfillment of the third commandment, the breaking of which is a grave sin requiring a good sacramental confession. This is why the Church can profess the truth about the importance of going to Mass—and the spiritual penalty for ignoring this fundamental command of God.

47. You mentioned that one should not receive the Eucharist in a state of mortal sin. Why not?

There cannot be a disconnect between what we do at a party on Friday night and what we do at Mass on Sunday morning. The Eucharist demands a whole way of life from us. A "Eucharistic life" is one lived in gratitude to God, in community with others, in purity of heart, and in service to the poor—in short, a life lived in union with and in imitation of the God who becomes the Eucharist for us. Mass is not about fulfilling a "to do" on our weekly calendar. It is about entering more deeply into a relationship with Jesus, "[who] is not just a private conviction or an abstract idea, but a real person who poured out His life for you."[27]

Pope Benedict continues: "At the beginning of the fourth century, Christian worship was still forbidden by the imperial authorities (in North Africa). Some Christians in North Africa, who felt bound to celebrate the Lord's Day, defied the prohibition. They were martyred after declaring that it was not possible for them to live without the Eucharist."[28] Even their deaths were Eucharistic, as they gave up their bodies for the One who gave up His body for them. Though our faith in Jesus in the Eucharist may not demand that we die, it does demand nothing less than our whole lives.

We all need to strive to make our whole lives reflect the mysteries we celebrate on Sunday morning. At a minimum, we should not compromise by living a double life. We cannot, for example, drive drunk on Saturday night and then receive Jesus worthily in the Eucharist the next morning (see CCC 2290). Doing so merely follows one wrong with another. Should we find ourselves in a state of mortal sin, we need to get to confession as soon as possible. Only then can we be certain that we are properly disposed to receive Jesus in the Eucharist. (*Note*: Many parishes, in addition to their regular Saturday afternoon and even weekday evening confession times, offer confession at scheduled times immediately before some of their Sunday morning Masses.)

48. Should parents force their children to go to Mass?

If a child wanted only to eat a steady diet of McDonald's fries and nothing else, should his parents "force" him to eat fruit and vegetables? Of course. Should they "force" him to go to school even if he doesn't want to? Absolutely. He has an obligation to society to make something of himself. And if parents are negligent in making sure he ate properly or went to school, he could be taken away from them and put into foster care. So why should parents take their obligations to God any less seriously?

Parents should try to convince their son or daughter of the value of worshiping God and hope that, in time, he or she will "get it" and choose to go to Mass on their own. If, however, they resist, it is a parent's responsibility to make sure their children do what is good for them, at least until they are eighteen or are living on their own.

So, should parents shame children into practicing their Catholic faith? No, but a little guilt is perfectly healthy.

Your child should know that he *should* feel bad when he fails to give God His due, just as he should when he fails at justice toward any person. Guilt can indicate when we have done something wrong. Losing a healthy sense of guilt is like anesthetizing one's conscience, which is very dangerous spiritually.

We suggest that parents not only require Mass attendance for minor children living under their roof, but that they also encourage them to become active in their parish or local Catholic youth group or go on a youth retreat, or both. Thanks to the concerted efforts of their parents, many teens and young adults have truly encountered Christ through such experiences, which led them to the deep, enriching relationship with Our Lord to which we are all called.

Chapter 4

HISTORY AND CHANGES

49. **What did the Mass look like in the earliest days of Christianity?**

Though the essentials never change, some of the "externals" of the Mass can change throughout time to help people in every age more effectively enter into the eternal mystery of the death and resurrection of Christ. Still, the Mass that the very first Christians celebrated looked a lot like it does today.

Early Christian worship is described in a letter written by a second-century martyr named Justin (c. A.D. 100–165). In the following excerpt, we find the same elements that we see in the modern Catholic Mass: readings from Scripture, a homily, petitions from the priest ("presider") and laity, the presentation of the gifts at the altar, a Eucharistic prayer, the great Amen, reception of Holy Communion, the Eucharist being brought to the sick, and a faith in the real presence of Jesus in the Eucharist.

> On the day called Sunday, all who live in cities or in the country gather together to one place, and the memoirs of the apostles or the writings of the prophets are read, as long as time permits; then, when the reader has ceased, the presider verbally

instructs, and exhorts to the imitation of these good things. Then we all rise together and pray ... when our prayer is ended, bread and wine and water are brought, and the presider in like manner offers prayers and thanksgivings, according to his ability, and the people assent, saying Amen; and there is a distribution to each, and a participation of that over which thanks have been given, and to those who are absent a portion is sent by the deacons.

We have been taught that the food which is blessed by the prayer of His word, and from which our blood and flesh ... are nourished, is the flesh and blood of that Jesus who was made flesh.[29]

Also check out Acts 2:42, where we see the Church gathering, listening to the teaching of the apostles, and breaking bread. If this all sounds familiar, it is because you have surely experienced such things many times at Mass.

50. **What are some of the major changes in the Mass over the past 2,000 years? Why did these come about?**

The mystery of the Mass itself is a gift from God. Because of this, at its core it never changes. The way in which we celebrate it (e.g., the prayers recited, the music sung, the candles and incense used, the colored vestments worn, etc.), though, has been refined over time, and we can see the "guidance of the Holy Spirit in this rich history" of the liturgy.[30]

In the words of Vatican II, the way in which we celebrate certain aspects of the Mass "not only may, but ought to be changed with the passage of time,"[31] though not in a way that is complete break with the past. Why should these changeable aspects of the Mass change over time? Because Jesus didn't just tell the Church to "go teach and baptize" (see Mt 28:19-20), but to "go, make disciples of the whole world" (Mt 28:19). In other words, go and "teach and present the sacraments *effectively*," i.e., in a way that actually converts hearts. For example, if we never changed the way in which we celebrated the Mass, it would still be celebrated in Jesus' language, Aramaic, only in small upper rooms, and with groups of twelve men. So, aspects of how the Mass is celebrated must change in order to reach people in different circumstances.

In the early Church, the Mass followed the same basic structure it does today. People gathered, readings were proclaimed, preached, and reflected on. Gifts were brought forward. Prayers were said. Bread and wine were changed into the Eucharist. Then people received Jesus in Holy Communion. Also, many rituals, such as the reading of psalms, kneeling, standing, the sign of peace, and praying words like "amen" and "alleluia" were directly carried over from Jewish worship into the early Church and remain in the Mass today. In those days, though, there were no set prayer books. We should assume that the Mass in the early Church would have been rather simple, since the Church was poor and persecuted. Since there were no set prayer books, the priest would have known the basic structure and likely would have "ad-libbed" some of the prayers.

The use of prayer books, more elaborate rituals, beautiful vestments, and sacred vessels developed after it became legal to publicly practice the Catholic faith in the early fourth century and congregations started to grow in numbers and in wealth. Over the ensuing several hundred years, the Church collected and organized the prayers, music, and readings that were to be used at Mass and designated Latin as the official language for the Roman Rite of the Catholic

Church. (There are other equally Catholic rites that have their own style of worship, such as the Byzantine Rite.)

The Mass of the Roman Rite did not change much from the early seventh-century until the 1960s, though it was refined following the Council of Trent (1545-1563) by St. Pius V (1566-1572) and subsequent popes. In the 1960s, in an effort to make sure she was still effectively reaching a rapidly changing world, the Church made significant changes to the rituals of the Mass. At the Second Vatican Council, the world's bishops called for liturgical renewal, authorizing changes to many of the prayers and rituals of the Mass so as to make them simpler and easier for anyone to grasp.[32] One significant change was to allow a greater use of the *vernacular* (i.e., the language of the people of a particular region) at Mass to facilitate the participation of the laity. This led to the almost universal use of the vernacular we see today.

A significant change to the Mass occurred in 2011. An entirely new English translation of the Mass was implemented with the publication of the *Third Edition of the Roman Missal*. The previous translation, in use since the early 1970s, utilized a "dynamic equivalence" approach that communicated the general meaning of the official Latin text of the Mass; the revised English version, however, is a more literal, word-for-word translation.

Today, the Mass more closely resembles descriptions of the Mass of the early Church than it has in more than a thousand years. The Church also now allows for more variety in the Mass depending on the locality and the abilities and needs of those who attend. We read the words of Vatican II: "Even in the Liturgy the Church does not wish to impose a rigid uniformity in matters which do not involve the Faith or the good of the whole community."[33] This is why one can hear Swahili and drums at a Mass in Africa, English and guitar at a Mass for teens in your home parish (even though the organ remains the official instrument of the Church), and a children's lectionary being read at a "children's Mass." The purpose of all liturgical options and adaptations is to help the people of God to enter into the unseen reality that is beyond particular languages and instruments. The Church even allows use of the Traditional Mass as it was celebrated before Vatican II—now officially called the Extraordinary Form of the Roman Rite—for those who experience a richer communion with God through it. As of September 14, 2007, any priest may celebrate Mass privately in the Extraordinary Form, and groups of lay people may petition their pastors to provide the Traditional Mass on a regular basis.

Despite the changes in the Mass over the centuries, many elements have remained constant, from specific prayers and vestments to the use of Latin and Gregorian chant. And the basic structure and the mystery that these rituals enfold is unchanging.

51. Who has authority to make changes in the Mass?

Since the Mass belongs to the entire Church and is such an important part of the "deposit of faith" (CCC 84) that comes down to us from the apostles, only the Magisterium (the official teaching authority of the Church) can authorize any changes to it. Not even a bishop has the right to change the official rite of the Mass on a whim.[34]

As we have pointed out, the heart of the Mass has remained the same ever since Jesus took bread into His hands at the Last Supper and said, "This is my body…" Every Mass since then has been the re-presentation of the Paschal Mystery (i.e., the death, resurrection, and ascension of Jesus).

Because the Church is presenting and joining in an action that is both human and divine—namely, the mystery of God the Son's eternal self-offering to God the Father—no one can change the core meaning or the basic structure of the Mass.[35] If we tried to change the Mass to mean something different at its core, taking away its sacrificial nature, it would no longer be the Mass. Because of this the Church has always been very conscious of guarding the prayers and rituals of the Mass, and if she makes any changes to the rites, she does so very carefully, lest we risk losing the essential meaning of the Mass over time and, thus, losing the Mass itself.

52. I once went to a "teen" Mass in which everyone gathered around the altar. Now I've heard that this is no longer permitted. Is this true?

Yes. According to the most recent edition of the *General Instruction of the Roman Missal (GIRM)*, issued in 2003, the practice of members of the congregation gathering around the altar is not allowed. While some may argue that such a practice has some benefit, at the end of the day, we must defer to the wisdom and the authority of the Church on all matters pertaining to the Mass. As Vatican II states, "the regulation of the sacred liturgy depends solely on the authority of the Church, which rests specifically with the Apostolic See and, according to the norms of law, with the bishop" (see *Sacrosanctum Concilium*, no. 22).

Despite the initial enthusiasm teens may experience, the practice of gathering around the altar at Mass might actually hurt their faith. In a self-centered culture that has generally lost a sense of reverence for what is sacred, we need reminders that some aspects of our faith, including the liturgy, are "set apart." In the Old Testament, for example, only the high priest could enter the Holy of Holies, the most sacred part of the temple. This is also why older Catholic churches used to have an altar rail that separated the congregation from the sanctuary.

As former youth ministers, the authors understand that gathering around the altar during Mass *could* have some positive effect on teens and young Catholics. But gathering young people around the altar, not as appropriately-vested Mass servers but as members of a youth group, emphasizes fellowship—a secondary element of Catholic worship—at the expense of reverence for the Holy Sacrifice of the Mass.

Chapter 5

MASS TERMS

53. My Protestant friend says that the word "Mass" is not in the Bible. Is he right?

I am sure that your non-Catholic friend means well, but he or she has a incorrect understanding of the Bible. The Bible is God's word, but it was never meant to be a dictionary of Christian terms or an exhaustive explanation of everything the Christian believer needs to know. It was never intended to be a catechism, which clearly and methodically lays out the doctrines of the faith. The Bible is a collection of writings or "books" which tell of salvation history—God's leading of a scattered people into (or back into) His family. The culmination of the Bible is the four gospels, accounts of the life and redeeming work of Jesus Christ. Everything before the gospels leads up to them. Everything after is commentary on them or application of them to specific communities and problems in the early Church (and to us today).

So, while not all Catholic terms (e.g., "Trinity", "Mass", "sacrament," etc.), some of which are also used by Protestants, are explicitly mentioned in the Bible, the truth expressed by a particular term can be found within its pages. The *word* "Mass" may not be in the Bible, but the *reality* of Mass is found throughout the New Testament.

54. I've heard that the word "Christmas" is related to the word "Mass." Is that true or just a coincidence?

It is true. The word *Christmas* comes from the Old English phrase "Cristes maesse"—in modern English, "Christ's mass." The earliest manuscript we know of that uses this phrase to describe the day of Christ's birth dates back to the year 1038. If you want to hang on to the real meaning of Christmas you need to keep Christ in Christmas. And if you want to keep Christ in Christmas, you need to keep the Mass in Christmas, too.

55. What does the word "Eucharist" mean?

Holy Eucharist is the official name for the sacrament of Christ's body and blood. While we commonly refer to the actual consecrated hosts that we receive in Holy Communion as "the Eucharist," the term is sometimes applied also to the Mass itself in which the sacrament is celebrated. "Eucharist" comes from the Greek word *eucharistein,* which literally means "to give thanks." It is applied to the Mass and the Blessed Sacrament because the celebration and reception of the Eucharist "is an action of thanksgiving to God" (CCC 1328).

The ultimate way to thank God for the amazing love He has poured out on us in Jesus Christ is to receive this love with a grateful receptivity. If you have ever loved someone, you know that the greatest gift is when that love is noticed, received, appreciated, and returned.

This is what we do at every Mass. At every Mass we call to mind how God has blessed us by creating, redeeming, and sanctifying us. That is why the readings at Mass usually start from the Old Testament and then move to the New Testament, giving us a "snapshot" of the big picture of salvation history. When we receive Jesus in the Eucharist, we are the recipients of the culmination of all that God has done for mankind since the beginning of time—making salvation history our own. Recognizing and receiving all of this awesome generosity with thankful hearts is a beautiful act of gratitude to God; hence the word *eucharistein*, which, again, means "to give thanks."

The Old Testament custom of offering a sacrifice to God in thanksgiving foreshadows the Mass: "How can I repay the LORD for all the good he has done for me? I will raise the cup of salvation and call on the name of the LORD" (Ps 116:12-13).

The Eucharist can also be seen as an act of thanksgiving offered on our behalf. What God the Father has done for us in Christ is far too great for us to ever repay it. God is infinite; He has no end and no equal. For Him to save us in Christ is an act of infinite generosity, which would require infinite gratitude. But we are finite. How can we offer Him the gratitude He deserves? We cannot. All we can do is "raise the cup of salvation" and offer Him what He has given us as a gift, His only Son. When we join our hearts to the heart of God the Son offering Himself to God the Father in the Eucharist, we are able to offer to the Father the thanks that He deserves.

While our intentions are important, and Jesus wants us to "cast our cares on him" (see 1 Pt 5:7), we need to always make sure we spend time thanking God after we receive

Holy Communion. We give thanks for the gift of our lives and the gift of eternal life that comes to us in Christ.

If we carry this "attitude of gratitude" with us all the time, we will be the "Eucharistic people" that God wants us to be. If we do, we will have the spirit of Venerable Solanus Casey, who suffered deeply but frequently said, "It's 'heaven begun,' for the grateful on earth."

56. You have used the term "liturgy" a few times. What does this word mean exactly?

The word *liturgy* comes from an ancient Greek term that means "a public work" or "a work on behalf of the people." As the *Catechism of the Catholic Church* says, "In Christian tradition it means the participation of the People of God in the work of God" (CCC 1069). In a broad sense, everything we do as Christians by the grace of God is "liturgy." In the stricter sense (and common use of the word) it refers to the official prayer of the Church.

Liturgy includes the celebration of all the sacraments, the liturgical year, the Liturgy of the Hours (the constant, corporate prayer of the Church, consisting of psalms, biblical canticles, and various readings), and most of all the Mass, which is sometimes called "the Divine Liturgy." Because it is the official prayer of the Church, liturgy is also the prayer of Jesus Christ, who is one with the Church as a head is one with its body. As important as personal prayer is, the Church's communal prayer with and through Jesus is the highest form of prayer. As the Church teaches in *Sacrosanctum Concilium*, Vatican II's Constitution on the Liturgy, "Every liturgical celebration, because it is an action of Christ the priest and of His body which is the Church, is a sacred action surpassing

all others; no other action of the Church can equal its
efficacy by the same title and to the same degree."[36]

Liturgy is the deepest prayerful "inter-action" of the
Church with Jesus Christ as we join ourselves to His
prayer—His eternal offering to the Father, in the Holy
Spirit. You might recognize a prayer said by every
priest around the world at Mass: "*Through Him, with
Him, in Him, in the unity of the Holy Spirit, all glory
and honor is Yours, almighty Father, forever and ever!*"
In the liturgy, everything we do as Christians is taken up
into Jesus' offering, and all the grace we live by as Christians
flows from it. That is why the liturgy "is the summit
towards which the activity of the Church is directed ...
[and] the font from which all her power flows."[37]

The liturgy also makes the story of the Bible the story of
our lives here and now. Through the liturgical celebration
of baptism, the waters prefigured by the Red Sea, the Flood,
and the River Jordan, and the water which flowed from
Christ's side, in a sense, converge on the head of the infant
as the redeeming work of God over thousands of years
becomes his. Through the liturgy, "especially in the divine
sacrifice of the Eucharist, 'the work of our redemption is
accomplished'"[38] as we receive His body given up for us.
Through the liturgical celebration of the sacrament of
confirmation, the story of Pentecost becomes the story of
a young person's life as he, like the apostles, is empowered
and sent forth by the Holy Spirit. Through the liturgical
year we live through the anticipation, birth, life, death, and
resurrection of Christ every year. The liturgy takes our
lives, here and now, and situates them in the context of the
big picture—salvation history, giving us the strength to do
our part in the work of God on earth today.

57. What is the purpose of the homily?

The homily during Mass is given by the priest or deacon after the Scripture readings. Its purpose is to help us to have a deeper understanding of the word of God so that it has a greater effect in our lives. "Homily" comes from the Greek word *homilein*, which means "to converse." Conversing implies more intimacy than just being "talked at" or lectured.

The Church teaches, "When the Sacred Scriptures are read in the Church, God himself speaks to his people."[39] The homily helps us to know how to respond to the word of God—making the Liturgy of the Word into a true conversation between God and His people.

58. What does "alleluia" mean?

The word *alleluia* is an ancient call to give praise to God. It comes from two Hebrew words *'allelu* and *yah* ("Yah" being a short form of "Yahweh," the personal name of God revealed to Moses at the burning bush), which literally means, "Praise the Lord!"

59. We say "amen" a lot during the Mass. What is the meaning of this word?

Amen is a Hebrew word meaning "truly." It is a way of affirming something we heard or said. When we say "Amen" at the end of a prayer we are saying "So be it!"—or as the Beatles so eloquently put it, "Let it be!"

When we sing the "Great Amen" at the conclusion of the Eucharistic Prayer, following the elevation of the consecrated host and chalice, we are affirming our belief in the power of the Eucharistic sacrifice of Christ and of His Real Presence in the Holy Eucharist.

60. What is the "tabernacle"?

The word *tabernacle* comes from the Latin for "tent," which refers to the tent in the Old Testament that was used to house the Ark of the Covenant as the Jews traveled for forty years through the desert. The Hebrew word for "tabernacle" is *mishkan*, which simply means "dwelling." This sacred space was considered the dwelling place of God. The Ark of the Covenant contained the tablets of the Ten Commandments; manna, which is the bread that came from heaven and fed the Jews as they wandered through the desert; and the staff of the high priest Aaron. (If you saw the first Indiana Jones movie, *Raiders of the Lost Ark*, you may remember this.) These three objects symbolize the word of God (the Ten Commandments), the bread from heaven (the manna; see also Jn 6:38), and the priesthood. It is no coincidence that these Old Testament objects also prefigure the elements of the Catholic Mass.

For the Jews wandering through the desert, the tabernacle was the holiest place in the universe. God dwelt there. (See Ex 25:22, 40:34-38 and Num 9:15-17.) Clouds and fire rested on it signifying God's holy presence. God told Moses to meet Him in the tabernacle where He would speak with him. He also told him to always leave the "bread of the presence" there before Him (see Ex 25:22), which is a foreshadowing of the Eucharist.

For Christians, the tabernacle is the "dwelling" place of Jesus in the Eucharist. Its original purpose was simply to store the Eucharist from Mass that was to be brought to those who could not attend Mass (usually because of

sickness). As the Church's understanding of Jesus' true
presence in the Eucharist deepened over time, however,
the tabernacle also became more and more important for
prayer and adoration (CCC 1379). This is why the Church
stipulates that it needs to be in a prominent place and be
beautifully adorned (see *Code of Canon Law*, 938).

There is a beautiful tabernacle at the diocesan center of the
Diocese of La Crosse, Wisconsin, with the words inscribed
on it, "He whom the world cannot contain, love imprisons
here." We should visit churches often and sit before Jesus
in the tabernacle where His powerful love, waiting for us,
can transform our hearts. (Or better yet, if your parish
offers Eucharistic adoration, go and meet Him there.)

Speaking of this love, St. Josemaria Escriva said, "When
you approach the tabernacle remember that He has been
waiting for you for twenty centuries."[40] As Pope John
Paul II wrote, "In the Eucharistic presence He remains
mysteriously in our midst as the one who loved us and
gave Himself up for us."[41] Despite his amazingly busy
schedule, he used to visit Jesus in the Blessed Sacrament
about twenty times each day. No wonder he was so full of
love and holiness. It is true that we often become like those
we hang out with.

A beautiful thing to contemplate is that, since we have the
Holy Spirit living in us through baptism and confirmation,
we are, in a sense, living tabernacles—dwelling places of
God (see 1 Cor 6:19-20). This is more true than ever
after we receive Jesus worthily in Holy Communion. This
means that we need to treat ourselves and those around
us with great reverence and dignity—just as we would a
tabernacle.

61. I've sometimes heard the words "Kyrie eleison" at the beginning of Mass. What does this phrase mean?

The words *Kyrie, eleison* is ancient Greek for "Lord, have mercy." At Mass we sometimes use this phrase during the penitential rite at the beginning of the Mass in which we acknowledge our sinfulness and ask God for His mercy. This recognition of our need for God's mercy and of His unfailing love and generosity toward us is essential to worship—which is, in large part, simply a recognition of who God is and who we are in His sight.

Those exact words have been prayed throughout the Church (both in the Roman Rite and in liturgies of Eastern Rite Catholics and Orthodox Christians) since the very beginning of Christianity. There are writings dating back to the fourth century that testify to the use of this beautiful and simple phrase at the Mass.

At Mass we often echo the priest, praying (and often singing) "Kyrie eleison, Christe eleison, Kyrie eleison." It is prayed three times, addressing the Trinity: God the Father, Son, and Holy Spirit.

62. You mentioned the word "consecration" earlier. Could you tell me more about what that means?

To consecrate something is to set it aside for a higher purpose. A building can be set aside as a memorial, though in a secular context the word usually used is "dedicate." In the religious sense, "to consecrate" means to set something aside for the worship and service of God, almost always through some sort of ritual.

Not only things but people are consecrated to God. When a man becomes a priest at ordination or a person enters religious life by taking vows (i.e., becomes a religious sister or brother), we can say that he or she is "consecrated." They belong more exclusively to God and the Church. In a sense, a married couple is consecrated, since each spouse is set aside exclusively for the other (imaging the union of Christ and His Church) and becomes a vessel of sacramental grace for the other. In fact, every Christian is consecrated to God and made sacred by the sacraments of initiation—baptism, confirmation, and Holy Eucharist—which "initiate" us into the life Jesus Christ, fill us with divine life, and make us part of His Church.

So holiness is not just for priests and religious (though they have a particularly beautiful and special calling). *You* belong to God. Did you know that you were that sacred? St. Paul even likens the average Christian to a Church building or a tabernacle. In his first letter to the Corinthians, he writes: "Do you not know that your body is a temple of the Holy Spirit within you, whom you have from God, and that you are not your own? For you have been purchased at a price" (1 Cor 6:19-20). And, in the letter to the Romans, he states, "None of us lives for oneself, and no one dies for oneself. For if we live, we live for the Lord, and if we die, we die for the Lord; so then, whether we live or die, we are the Lord's" (Rom 14:7-8).

In the Mass, the word "consecration" refers to the ritual in which the bread and wine that have been set aside for a sacred purpose are changed into the body and blood of Christ. The consecration occurs when the priest holds the host and pronounces the words: "Take this, all of you, and eat it: this is my body which will be given up for you." And then, holding the cup, he says: "Take this, all of you, and drink from it: this is the cup of my blood, the blood of the new and everlasting covenant. It will be shed for you and for all so that sins may be forgiven. Do this in memory of me." The bread and wine are consecrated and become Jesus Christ so that you can be more deeply consecrated to God.

63. Why is the use of Latin encouraged by the Church when people do not understand what is being said?

From about the fifth century to the mid-1960s, most of the Mass of the Roman Rite of the Catholic Church (with the exception of the homily and a few words from ancient Greek and Hebrew) was celebrated in Latin. A large percentage of the non-Latin speaking world that converted to Christianity joined the "Latin Rite," which celebrated the liturgy in Latin. After Vatican II the use of the vernacular (i.e., the language of the people) was permitted so as to help people more fully understand and participate in the Mass. This change was a great blessing to many people. Today, while most of the Mass is said in the vernacular, the use of at least some Latin at Mass is still encouraged and is often heard—and it is still perfectly legitimate to have the entire Mass said in Latin. In several of his addresses Pope Benedict XVI has reminded us of the importance of preserving Latin in the prayer life of the Church.[42]

Latin is the official language of the Roman Catholic Church. The use of this ancient language in prayer is one way we remember our heritage as Roman Catholics and express unity with other Roman Catholics around the world and throughout history. Just as people remember and use their native languages even after they move to a new country, so the Western Church has not forgotten her mother tongue, and we should not be afraid to use it appropriately in worship, in accordance with the Church's official documents on the liturgy.

64. I've heard that the phrase "hocus pocus" referring to magic was originally used as a mockery of the Mass. Is this true?

This does seem to be the case. The words of consecration in Latin are: *Hoc est enim corpus meum*, which means "This is my body." Many believe that the phrase "hocus pocus" is a distortion of these words, used to mock the Mass and the Catholic doctrine of "transubstantiation," equating it with belief in a silly magic trick. John Tillotson, the Anglican archbishop of Canterbury, wrote in 1694 that the phrase was "in all probability" a mockery of the Mass. So that may be the origin of "hocus pocus," but there is no conclusive proof that this is the case. This brings up another great question, though: What is the difference between believing in the consecration and believing in a magic trick?

A miracle of God is a far cry from a magic trick, and a claim of a magician is a far cry from a claim made by Jesus Christ. If a magician doing a card trick said it was not a trick but was real you would assume he was joking. If he continued to insist it was real, you would think he was crazy. If the magician legitimized his claims by countless miracles, though—the most impressive of which was rising from the dead—you would likely come believe to him. This exactly what Jesus did. It is because of Christ's resurrection that we can be sure that the words *hoc est enim corpus meum* ("this is my body") is more than a trick—it is the truth.

Chapter 6

MINISTERS OF THE MASS

65. During the consecration at Mass, why does the priest say "this is *my* body" rather than "this is Jesus' body"?

Because, after receiving the sacrament of holy orders, a priest does not say those words on his own, but as a man standing *in persona Christi*, i.e., "in the person of Christ."

Jesus remains with us in tangible ways in the sacraments. Two sacraments, considered the "sacraments at the service of communion" (see CCC, part two, chapter three), require people to be the sign and symbol that God transforms into a vessel of his grace: marriage, in which God comes to a husband through his wife, and a wife through her husband; and holy orders, in which God comes to His Church through the priest. Holy orders is one of the beautiful ways that Jesus Christ remains with His Church.

Those who receive this sacrament through ordination are consecrated, or "set aside," for the worship of God and the service of the Church. A youth minister who is a layperson can leave his job to become a circus performer or a business executive. "Youth minister" is what he *does*, not who he *is*. If that same layperson is a husband and father, this position is more than a job he does; it is his vocational state in life. "Husband" and "father" describe who he *is*. Likewise, for the priest, ministry is not his job but his vocation. The sacrament of holy orders made a permanent change in his soul, giving him a unique power received from Jesus Christ for ministry (see CCC 1538, 1570).

Every Catholic, by virtue of baptism, participates in the "apostolate" or apostolic work of the Church, each in his or her own way. The Catholic priest, however, is set apart by his ordination with a unique power for ministry (see CCC 1120, 1552). When a priest receives holy orders he no longer ministers in his own name or by his own particular gifts and charisms; rather, he ministers "in the person of Christ" (*in persona Christi*).

This is technical, theological terminology for the fact that it is not just the particular bishop, priest, or deacon ministering when he administers the sacraments, preaches, and serves the Church at the liturgy and in charitable work. Rather, it is Jesus Himself ministering through the ordained man. Because of this, the priest does not say, "This is *Jesus'* body," but, "This is *my* body." And when hearing confessions, he does not say, "Jesus absolves you from your sins," but "*I* absolve you" (see CCC 1120, 1552).

How can the Church make such a radical claim about her ministers? It is clear that Jesus established a priesthood of the New Covenant in the apostles. It is also clear that Jesus is the final high priest and the only one of the New Covenant. How do we reconcile these two realities? The only explanation is that a priest shares in the one priesthood of Jesus Christ, who works in and through him to minister to His people. In one sense, there aren't many individual priests, but many who share in the one priesthood of Jesus (see CCC 1545).

This claim of the Church should not shock us. At the next baptism you attend, listen and watch closely as the baby is anointed a priest, prophet, and king. Though their priesthood is "essentially different" than that of the ordained, all the baptized share in Christ's priesthood and are called to be intercessors for the world and to offer God the sacrifice of their daily lives (CCC 1547; see also 1141, 1268). Furthermore, it is not uncommon to encounter God moving in our lives in powerful ways through other people. God has always done amazing things through people— like making other people, for instance! Or consider how He came into the world through a humble, teenage girl. Mary said, "He that is mighty has done great things for me, and holy is His name" (Lk 1:49). God loves to use lowly creatures as a way to pour out blessings upon His people. This is a fundamental rule in our sacramental life as Catholics; the priesthood is a striking example of it.

As St. John Vianney, the patron saint of parish priests, puts it, "The priest continues the work of redemption on earth ... If we really understood the priest on earth, we would die not of fright but of love ... the Priesthood is the love of the heart of Jesus" (quoted in CCC 1589).

66. Is a Mass still valid if the priest is in a state of mortal sin?

Suppose that your local parish priest was thrown in jail for extortion. You may wonder, then: Were the babies that he baptized over the past ten years really baptized? Were those who made their confessions to him in the sacrament of reconciliation really forgiven by God? Were the Masses that he celebrated valid? Absolutely. Not by his merits and not for his sake, but for ours.

Recent experiences have reminded us that a priest is still very human and part of the larger human population. Therefore, it is logical to assume that at any given time a certain percentage of our priests are struggling with sin. A certain very small percentage may even have extreme personality disorders and commit very grave sins (though there are now more safeguards in place in the Church than in just about any other institution to screen out potentially problematic seminarians and priests and thus to protect the flock). But it is not a clergyman's holiness or lack thereof that gives him the supernatural ability to confer the sacraments. It is the holiness of Jesus Christ working through him by virtue of the sacrament of holy orders.

When we receive a sacrament, it isn't about us encountering Father So-and-so. It is about encountering Jesus Christ, who is the primary Person acting in our lives through a particular sacrament. St. Augustine gives us the analogy that a vessel (i.e., a container), whether it is made of gold or rusty metal, will still carry water effectively. Just so, regardless of the quality of the priest, God will work through him to reach us with the sacraments. The priest does not even have to believe in the Eucharist in order to consecrate it, because the Mass is not dependent upon the priest's personal faith either. He only has to intend to do the actions the Church tells him to do (see CCC 1128).

Why would Jesus place Himself into the hands of an unbelieving priest or a priest who is in sin? For the same reason that He allowed Himself to be handed over to those who crucified Him—out of love for us. We can be sure that when we go to Mass, Jesus will be there for us, whether the priest seems to love Him or not!

If a priest is in mortal sin, he should go to confession before celebrating the sacraments (just as we should before receiving the Eucharist), unless he has a grave reason not to (e.g., he could not get to confession and a parishioner needs confession, or to avoid scandalizing people, or it is time to celebrate Mass and five hundred people are in church waiting). In that case, he should pray for forgiveness and plan to get to confession as soon as he is able (see *Code of Canon Law*, 916 and 1352).

67. What is the difference between a priest and a deacon? And what is the deacon's role at Mass?

The sacrament of holy orders, which is only one sacrament, has three "rungs" or "degrees." The ordained minister stands "in the person of Christ" as he serves the Church but this ministry manifests itself in different ways, depending on the degree of his ordination (see CCC 1554).

A bishop, who occupies the highest "degree" of holy orders and is a successor to the apostles (see the "ordination" of Matthias to the apostolic ministry in Acts, chapter one), has received the fullness of this sacrament. He is an image to us of Jesus, the Good Shepherd. A good symbol of the bishop is the *crosier* (i.e., shepherd's staff) he carries in liturgical processions. He is the shepherd (i.e. pastor or leader) of the flock that resides in his diocese. As such, the bishop is the chief teacher and governor of his diocese and is able to celebrate all the sacraments, including the ordination of men to the priesthood.

A priest is an "extension" of the bishop and works under him to serve the spiritual needs of the people of his parish, including bringing them the sacraments. A good symbol for a priest is the Eucharist. He is an image to us of Jesus at the Last Supper, sharing Jesus' life and sacraments with His people. He can administer all of the sacraments except for holy orders (though the ordinary minister of confirmation in the Roman Rite is the bishop; see CCC 1313).

A deacon, who has a direct and special connection to his bishop, is ordained for a ministry of service. The word *diakonos* is an ancient Greek term meaning "servant." A good image to contemplate when thinking of a deacon is Jesus washing the feet of the apostles at the Last Supper. A deacon is ordained for the service of the altar, of the Word, and of charity (see CCC 1596). See Acts 6 to read about the ordination of the first deacons to serve the needs of the poor. In the Scriptures, we can see some development in the particular duties of deacons, though charity remains at the heart of their ministry. Though a deacon does not have the ability to consecrate the Eucharist, hear confessions, or anoint the sick as can a priest, he does properly assist at Mass, proclaim the Gospel, preach, preside at funerals and weddings, and baptize.

Some older Catholics found it a challenge getting used to married deacons. In the Roman rite, a married man is eligible to be ordained to the diaconate (but not to the priesthood). No ordained man, though, is eligible to receive the sacrament of marriage. Canon law, both in the Roman rite and also in the Eastern Churches, regards any degree of holy orders as an "impediment" (or legal obstacle) to entering marriage. A married man may devote himself to God's service as a deacon, with his wife's consent. An ordained man, however, cannot give himself to a woman as a husband, because he is no longer entirely his own to give.

At Mass, you can visibly distinguish a deacon from a priest by the stole worn diagonally over one shoulder, whereas a priest's stole hangs around his neck over both shoulders. Liturgically, the deacon's role is very simple and humble. He stands to the side and slightly behind the priest, assisting him with things such as the holding up the chalice during the doxology at the end of the Eucharistic Prayer (i.e., immediately before the Great Amen). Aside from when he acts in his role as "servant of the Word," proclaiming the Gospel and preaching the homily, he speaks very little, reading the intercessions and giving a few directives to the congregation (e.g., inviting the exchange of the sign of peace and offering the dismissal at the end of Mass, "Go in peace"). As mentioned previously, a deacon cannot consecrate the Eucharist and, although on other occasions he can offer a blessing, the priest gives the final blessing at Mass.

68. Why do bishops, priests, and deacons wear medieval-looking outfits?

It is typical in the secular world for those who have important roles to wear distinctive outfits. This is true in the sacred world of the Church as well. A priest's vestments are no more a "medieval costume" than are a judge's robe or a college professor's graduation gown. They are outfits that express the importance of their respective roles. Distinctive attire for religious leaders is common in nearly every faith, from the major world religions to the primitive religions. As body-soul composites, people have an innate need to express invisible realities in tangible, physical ways. Special garb for religious leaders is one of those ways.

Actually, priestly vestments are far older than the Middle Ages. In the Roman Rite, the vestments that the priest wears while celebrating the sacraments have their origins in the garb of ancient Rome.

The white robe worn by those in holy orders is called an *alb*. It resembles a Roman tunic, which was once commonly worn, and is a symbol of baptism. While the world changed its common dress, the priest's garb has remained the same and came to denote his sacred duty. As a symbol of baptism, an alb is worn to indicate holiness and purity (which is why we put babies in all-white outfits when they are baptized).

The *stole* is the long cloth that hangs over a priest's neck and down over his shoulders like a long scarf. A deacon's stole, by comparison, drapes diagonally across his chest. A stole is a symbol of authority (i.e., the "yolk of Christ"; see Mt 11:30) and is believed to have originated in the garb worn by a Roman judge.

The *chasuble* is the outermost garment that the priest wears that often has a cross embroidered on the back. It comes from the Latin word, *casula*, meaning, "little house." The color of the chasuble worn for at Mass depends on the liturgical feast day or season that the Church is celebrating (see question 37).

In addition to the above-mentioned vestment, a bishop wears a cross, a ring, a skull cap (known as a *zucchetto*), a crosier (his shepherd's staff), and a *mitre*, the double pointed hat symbolizing the Old and New Testaments which he is commissioned to teach. An archbishop also wears a band of white wool around his called a *pallium*. It is placed on him by the pope on the Feast of St. Peter and

Paul as a sign of his appointment by the Holy Father to oversee the Church in his particular region.

So, the distinctive dress of those in holy orders helps us to recognize both the high and sacred state of our ministers, to enter more fully into the sublime nature of our worship, and to see the link of our faith today with that of the early Church.

69. Why can only a priest or deacon read the Gospel and preach the homily the Mass?

The proclamation of the Gospel and the homily that follows are not just a spiritual reading and a nice reflection, but are an integral part of the Mass. Because of this, they are actions of God Himself. The Mass is different from any other "prayer service" (even a communion service). As we have discussed, the sacred Liturgy is a work of God. Listen to this beautiful quote from the *General Instruction of the Roman Missal*: "When the Sacred Scriptures are read in the Church, God himself speaks to His people, and Christ, present in His own word, proclaims the Gospel."[43]

The Gospel is set apart from the other readings because it is the culmination and center of the entire Bible, where God is most fully revealed through His own words and actions in Christ. Through the Gospel, Jesus Christ reveals Himself to us here and now—not just in the words being read, but in the reading of those living words. It is Jesus proclaiming and sharing Himself with us, a sharing that He completes by sharing Himself in the Eucharist. Just as an ordained minister, who stands "in the person of Christ" (see questions 14, 25, 65, 72, 87), is necessary for Jesus to give us the Eucharist at the consecration, it is also most fitting that a person who stands in the person of Christ proclaim the word as Jesus shares Himself with us in the Gospel and homily at Mass.

70. By the way, why can't women be priests?

Before answering this question, it is important to remember nobody has a "right" to be ordained to the priesthood. No one "deserves" ordination. The sacrament of holy orders is not given to honor any particular individual. It is a gift from God for the good and service of the whole Church.

The *Catechism of the Catholic Church* gives a very simple reason why the Church chooses only men for this sacrament. We follow the example of Jesus who only chose men to be His apostles and share in His priesthood: "The Church recognizes herself to be bound by this choice made by the Lord Himself. For this reason the ordination of women is not possible" (CCC 1577).

Why did Jesus choose only men to be his apostles? Be assured that it was for the most profound theological reasons, not because of male chauvinism or the social customs of His day.

We can be sure that Jesus' decision was not due to pressures from the society in which He lived, because Jesus made the ultimate sacrifice for the truth that He proclaimed. Had He been concerned about what his contemporaries wanted, He would not have proclaimed His teachings unto death. Jesus proclaimed some radical things, including that He Himself was God. To include women as part of His ministry would have been far less scandalous than that, especially to a group of people who so reverenced God that they would not even say His name. In addition, the idea of a female priesthood would not have been foreign to Jesus or the people of His day. There were plenty of priestesses in the pagan religions of ancient world.

Nor can we attribute Jesus' decision not to ordain women to a low view of women or to a lack of suitable candidates. The holiest person in the history of the Church (and, indeed, the world) was a woman, His own Mother, Mary. Her perfect and unwavering faith in following Jesus from the beginning until the bitter end revealed a holiness and courage greater than that of all the apostles. Nevertheless, Mary wasn't chosen for the sacrament of holy orders.

Perhaps Jesus' choice of men for this sacrament was purely a sacramental issue. As we discussed in question 13, a sacrament is a sign that makes what it symbolizes actually happen. God uses the material world to reach the material people He created. If the proper physical symbol (i.e., the proper *matter*, in sacramental terms) is not present, the sacrament will not happen. If birthday cake and milk were used at Mass instead of bread and wine (symbols of body and blood), the sacrament of the Eucharist simply would not happen. In the sacrament of holy orders, the proper symbol is a man who stands "in the person of Christ." It matters that the priest be a male because he is standing in the person of Jesus Christ, the Bridegroom of the Church.

In light of these truths, the Church continues to honor Jesus' choice of men for the sacrament of holy orders.

71. **If women cannot be priests, why are female altar servers permitted in many places?**

Though it can be a great recruiting ground for priestly vocations, being an altar server is not necessarily linked to becoming a priest. Either sex can serve in many different ways at Mass, including being an altar server.

Some dioceses in the United States have retained the custom of allowing only boys or men to serve at the altar. Whether or not altar servers go "coed" is not a question of right or wrong, but rather of what, in the pastoral judgment of a bishop, works best for his diocese in helping to spread the Gospel. Since the mid-1990s, the Vatican has allowed the local bishop to make the decision on whether or not to permit female altar servers in his diocese. And, even if a bishop decides he will allow female altar servers, an individual pastor may decide not to employ that option in his parish.

Female altar servers are now allowed throughout most of the English-speaking world. Those bishops and priests who choose to allow girls to serve at the altar usually say that it is a great opportunity to re-affirm the role of women in the apostolate (i.e., mission) of the Church. Those who have chosen to remain with male altar servers often remark that it is a great source of recruitment for the priesthood and a good way to reach out to boys whose attendance at Mass may be slipping. Some young boys, due to peer pressure, may not want to be a part of something that they see girls doing. A parish and/or diocese has to consider this social reality as they make pastoral plans. Because of the many local factors to consider, the Vatican has left this decision to Church leaders at the local level.

72. What is the proper role of altar servers at Mass?

Altar servers have a beautiful and important job. Pope John Paul II, speaking to altar servers in Rome on August 1, 2001, said, "Jesus ... acts through the priest who celebrates Holy Mass and administers the sacraments *in persona Christi.* Therefore in the liturgy you are far more than mere 'helpers of the parish priest.' Above all, you are servants of Jesus Christ, the eternal High Priest." So, simply, the job of an altar server is to be a helper of Jesus Christ in simple ways (e.g., lighting candles, ringing bells, etc.) during His most intimate encounter with His people, the Mass.

Their job is also a privilege for them and a call from God to deeper intimacy with Him. In the words of John Paul, at Mass, "they experience from close at hand that Jesus Christ is present and active in every liturgy." They are "called to be young friends of Jesus. [To] [s]trive to deepen this friendship with him."

73. **A friend told me that only priests and deacons should distribute the Eucharist at Mass. What about the Eucharistic ministers I see every Sunday?**

Ordained ministers—bishops, priests, and deacons— who stand "in the person of Christ" for us, are the most fitting people to give us Jesus in the Eucharist at Mass because they, themselves, are a sacramental sign of Jesus giving Himself to His people, just as He did at the Last Supper and on the Cross. Thus, those in holy orders are the ordinary ministers of communion (see *Code of Canon Law*, no. 910).

However, the Church recognizes that circumstances will not always allow for the distribution of Holy Communion exclusively by ordained ministers. In those cases "extraordinary ministers" of the Eucharist may be used (see CCC 903). The most common reason for the use of extraordinary ministers is that there are too few ordained ministers to dispense the Eucharist in a timely fashion to a large number of communicants (e.g. the next Sunday Mass is scheduled right after this one, or communicants at a daily Mass might need to leave quickly to get to work on time). The Church does not provide detailed criteria for when to utilize extraordinary ministers of the Eucharist but leaves this decision to local pastors, who are expected to call upon extraordinary ministers only as needed.

Chapter 7

PRAYERS AND GESTURES

74. **My parish church is very ornate, with a lot of marble and beautiful statues. Why doesn't the Church just give the money it spends on such things to the poor?**

At first glance, this seems like a reasonable question, but there is more here than meets the eye. The short answer is that spending money to honor God is money well spent which also benefits the poor.

Think about it. We spend hundreds of millions of dollars to build arenas for sports teams and rock concerts, yet few complain about the social injustice of that. Why should we complain, then, if we spend a fraction of that cost to honor God? Scripture supports this notion of honoring God with our material possessions. After a woman "wasted" expensive perfume anointing Jesus' head, people protested, "Why has there been this waste of perfumed oil? It could have been sold for more than three hundred days' wages and the money given to the poor" (Mk 14:4-5). Evidently, Judas was especially upset; he went off to betray Jesus right after this incident. Jesus, of course, defended the woman saying, "Why do you make trouble for [her]? She has done a good thing for me … wherever this gospel is proclaimed in the whole world, what she has done will be spoken of, in memory of her" (Mt 26:10; 13).

What did Jesus teach that Judas missed? He taught that spending money to honor Him is in no way incompatible with spending money to care for the poor. Our money can be spent on both. And an investment in evangelization can even lead to more parishioners and therefore more donations to the poor.

Building a beautiful church is part of evangelization. It proclaims that the kingdom of God is here in a "concrete" way. It helps people enter into the worship of God. We are not disembodied spirits (like the angels). We are body-soul composites. We respond to the material world. When the material world is beautiful, we respond. When a church is beautiful, we respond.

The money invested in evangelization contributes to the conversion of souls, and converted souls mean more people loving and serving the poor. Statistics show that people who faithfully practice their religion generally do the most good for the poor.

Not surprisingly, many cathedrals, usually the most ornate churches in a diocese, are also centers of social service. Poor people constantly drop by seeking (and receiving) help. The Catholic Charities office is often located near the cathedral of a diocese, not only because the administrative center of the diocese is usually nearby, but because the cathedral is also a parish church to which many poor people are drawn to receive assistance.

Also, it is important to note that beautiful churches aren't just built for the rich, but for the poor as well. The poor, too, are inspired by the art, incense, music, and architecture of the Church. The poor, like everyone else, need more than material things. They need to have their hearts and minds lifted up to heaven for inspiration. Chances are, at any given time you will find poor (and even homeless) people walking around inside the cathedral of a large city. They need to be fed both physically and spiritually. It seems that the people who complain most about expensive churches and art usually are not poor at all.

75. Is it true that every altar in a Catholic church has the relics of a saint in it?

It is not required that an altar have a relic (i.e., bones) of a saint within or beneath it, but it is wonderful if it does. As the *General Instruction of the Roman Missal* states, "The practice of placing relics of saints, even those not martyrs, under the altar to be dedicated is fittingly retained. Care should be taken, however, to ensure the authenticity of such relics" (*GIRM*, no. 302).

This tradition dates from the earliest days of the Church when Mass was celebrated over the burial places of martyrs who gave up their lives for Christ. When the persecutions ended and the Church emerged (literally) from underground, these relics (bones) were often brought to the location for the altar in a new church building. St. Ambrose, who died in the year 397, wrote about this, "Let these triumphant victims be brought to the place where Christ is the victim. But He upon the altar, who suffered for all; they beneath the altar, who were redeemed by His Passion."[44]

The bones beneath the altar are a reminder, not of the power of the saints, but of the power of Jesus Christ to make saints out of us sinners. St. Augustine wrote, "It is not, then, the bodies of the martyrs that render the altar glorious; it is the altar that renders the burial place of martyrs glorious."[45]

This is a powerful reminder of the holiness that the Eucharist made possible for them, and makes possible for us. We tend to romanticize saints, as if it came naturally for them to be so holy, or as if it was easy for the early Christian martyrs to be eaten alive by lions for their faith. It wasn't. But Jesus, the source of our strength in the Eucharist, made this supernatural holiness possible for them, and He does the same for you to become Saint [*insert your name here*].

76. Why do we genuflect when we enter the church?

As mentioned previously, we humans are "body and soul composites." We do not simply display love, affection, joy, sadness, or even worship interiorly with our mind, but with our whole being. Contrary to what some non-Catholics may think, all of our "up and down" movements at Mass are not some new form of spiritual aerobics. Our body postures at Church have meaning and help our souls take the correct "posture" toward God.

Sitting is a sign that we are listening and learning, as we do in a classroom. This is our posture during the homily. Standing is a sign that we are actively attentive and respectful, as we see in a courtroom when the bailiff orders, "All rise," as the judge enters. Similarly, we stand at Mass to hear Jesus proclaimed in the Gospel.

It is only natural to show reverence with our bodies toward holy things. Some religions do this by removing their shoes or becoming silent when they enter a holy place. Even before the days when knights knelt before their king, kneeling and bowing were common ways for Roman Catholics to show humble reverence. This is why we kneel during the Eucharistic prayers (consecration, etc.) at Mass. Kneeling is a physical sign of our humble acknowledgement that we have entered into something way bigger than us. It is also why we genuflect (i.e., briefly kneeling on the right knee) toward the tabernacle and bow before the altar in church. There are no places in the universe more holy than the altar and the tabernacle, so it is only appropriate that we visibly show reverence to them when we enter the church or pass by them.

The altar is holy because it is a symbol of Jesus Christ Himself. As a sign of sacrifice, the altar is a sign of the cross, the place where God meets man in the person of Jesus. The altar is also holy because of what happens there. It is the most visible, central focal point of a Church because it is at the heart of the action in the liturgy. Because the central event of history, the Paschal Mystery (i.e., the death, resurrection, and ascension of Jesus that took place during and fulfilled the Passover) is re-presented there at Mass, the altar is also at the mystical center of time and space.

As Pope John Paul II has noted, "Even when it is celebrated on the humble altar of a country church, the Eucharist is ... celebrated on the altar of the world. It unites heaven and earth" (*Ecclesia de Eucharistia*, no. 8). For all these reasons we should bow reverently when passing in front of the altar.

We genuflect before the tabernacle when we enter a Church or when we pass in front of it because it not only symbolizes the presence of Christ to us, but because Jesus is present there, in the flesh, just as really as He was present to Mary and the apostles.

77. How does the Church select the Scripture readings at Mass?

The readings you hear at your church every day weren't chosen by your parish priest but were decided on in the years after the Second Vatican Council by the Congregation for Divine Worship. This Vatican office, using the authority given it by the pope, commissioned and approved our current Lectionary, the book containing the Scripture readings for each day of the liturgical calendar. Though the priest celebrant has a bit of leeway in his choice of readings for certain feast days and special occasions (such as weddings and funerals), for the most part, the readings on a given day are the same throughout the entire Roman Catholic Church. That means that if you went to Mass today, you heard the same readings that the pope read at Mass, and that a congregation in Zimbabwe heard. This is one of the many beautiful ways that we see the unity of the Catholic Church.

In general, the readings at each Mass fit thematically with liturgical seasons and specific feast days. There is a three-year cycle for the Sunday readings, and a two-year cycle for weekday readings. For Sundays, the Lectionary specifies an Old Testament reading, a responsorial psalm, a New Testament reading (usually from one of the "epistles" [or letters] of St. Paul or another apostle), and, finally, a passage from the Gospel. The Old Testament reading, psalm, and Gospel are selected so as to have a common theme, while the New Testament selection is read continuously from week to week, unless there is a special season or feast day. The readings at weekday Mass consist of a reading from either the Old or New Testament, the responsorial psalm, and, finally, the Gospel.

This cycle of readings ensures that we hear a representative sampling of Bible passages and not just those that are easy to preach on or that your pastor happens to like best. If you go to daily Mass you will hear readings from nearly every book of the Bible over the course of a year.

78. What exactly is the gesture we should make before the Gospel reading at Mass?

Before the Gospel is read, we offer a simple prayer that what we are about to hear doesn't just go in one ear and out the other. We do this by making a small sign of the cross with our right thumb on our forehead, lips, and heart, praying that God's word will be in our minds, on our lips, and in our hearts as we say aloud, "Glory to you, O Lord!" This beautiful prayer helps us to be attentive to the truths we are about to hear.

We must remember that, of all the words that fill our lives, there are none more important than the word of God being proclaimed. A Scripture reading at Mass is precisely that, and we should stop whatever we are thinking about and give it our full attention. Priests and theologians speak about God, but in Sacred Scriptures, God Himself speaks. The Scriptures were inspired in such a way that God is the "primary author," while the human writer was the "secondary author."[46] Who is more worth listening to than our Creator? And if we are attentive, we will not only hear His word, we will receive the grace to live it. Every time the Sacred Scriptures are proclaimed, life-transforming grace is given, "for the word of God is living and active, and sharper than any two-edged sword" (Heb 4:12).

We can even say that, in a mystical way, Jesus is present in His word being read at Mass and is proclaiming it to us in the priest who stands in the person of Christ. That is why, after listening to the Gospel we pray, "Praise to you, Lord Jesus Christ!"

Pope John Paul II had a wonderful sense of this reality. He *knew* Christ is present in His word. That's why he asked his friends to read John's gospel to him as he died. Often, after the Gospel was proclaimed at Mass, he would explain in his homily that Jesus was speaking to us here and now through His word. After reading the Gospel at World Youth Day 2002, he linked the voice of Christ spoken on a hillside near Galilee to the pilgrims gathered on a hillside near Lake Ontario saying, "On a hillside near the lake of Galilee, Jesus' disciples listened to His gentle and urgent voice ... The Lord spoke words of life that would echo for ever in the hearts of His followers ... Today He is speaking the same words to you ... Listen to the voice of Jesus in the depths of your hearts! His words tell you who you are as Christians. They tell you what you must do to remain in His love."[47] In the words of his successor, Pope Benedict, XVI, "Christ does not speak in the past, but in the present."[48]

God is speaking at Mass. Are you listening?

79.   Why do people in the RCIA program leave Mass after the homily?

For those who are not aware of RCIA, this is an abbreviation for the *Rite of Christian Initiation of Adults*. It is the ordinary process through which people are brought into the Church, whether they are from Protestant or non-

Christian backgrounds. (There is also RCIC, the *Rite of Christian Initiation of Children*.)

The practice of dismissing RCIA candidates from Church before the Eucharistic Prayer goes back to the first century of the Church. Persecution was so bad in the early Church that Christians tried to keep non-believers from finding out about their greatest of treasures, the Holy Eucharist, for fear that it would be mocked and desecrated. They did not even let the *catechumens* (i.e., unbaptized persons who were preparing to enter the Church) attend the entire Mass until they were baptized. Then, at the Easter Vigil Mass— which is the most solemn Mass of the year, commemorating the night when Jesus rose from the dead—the Church listened to readings that gave a panorama of salvation history, and then celebrated this history becoming present in the lives of those catechumens as they were baptized and confirmed. These new Christians then discovered that there was so much more to their initiation into the Church: they were now guests at a sacred banquet hosted by their Lord and Savior, Jesus Christ!

While catechumens and candidates entering the Church today learn about the Eucharist well before being initiated into the Church at the Easter Vigil, this practice of dismissing them from Sunday Mass after the Liturgy of the Word continues today. In many parishes they immediately go off to classes to help them prepare for that great gift that you already enjoy. Do not take it for granted.

80. Why do we shake hands at the sign of peace?

No good father could rest knowing that his children are not at peace with one another. That is why Jesus said, "If you bring your gift to the altar, and there recall that your brother has anything against you, leave your gift there at the altar, go first and be reconciled with your brother, and then come and offer your gift" (Mt 5:23-24). (Many other Scripture passages emphasize the importance of loving everyone, even our enemies.) God wants His people to be in communion with one another before we receive Him in Holy Communion.

Does that mean you have to "like" everyone, or that if you have an unresolved issue with someone you cannot receive Holy Communion? No. If it did mean that than, very likely, no one could ever receive the Eucharist. It does mean that, at the very least, you have to love everyone enough to be able to wish them the peace of Christ. According to St. Thomas Aquinas, to love someone is to will what is good for them. This is how you can love—even deeply—someone who drives you crazy. You can do good for them, forgive them in your heart (even if they have not apologized), wish them the peace of Christ, and pray for their salvation. Having this attitude of peace toward everyone is not easy, but it is liberating. It is also necessary if we are to call ourselves Christians. In the words of St. John,

> If anyone says, "I love God," but hates his brother, he is a liar; for whoever does not love a brother whom he has seen cannot love God whom he has not seen. This is the commandment we have from him: whoever loves God must also love his brother (Jn 4:20-21).

Peace in our hearts is the root of peace in the world. Only when we are truly at peace with others can we promote peace in the world around us. As followers of Christ we have an obligation to be "peacemakers" (Mt 5:9).

As Pope Benedict XVI teaches, "In our times, fraught with fear and conflict, this gesture [the sign of peace] has become particularly eloquent, as the Church has become increasingly conscious of her responsibility to pray insistently for the gift of peace and unity for herself and for the whole human family."[49] If every person on earth lived out what is signified by the sign of peace, all wars would end.

At the sign of peace, do not just think about those around you but about everyone in your life and wish them peace. Then come and offer the gift of yourself to Jesus.

81.   What is the symbolism of the offertory procession?

The offertory procession "enables us to appreciate how God invites man to participate" in His own work.[50] God wants us to participate in the work of bringing His kingdom to the world—in everything from teaching people about Him, to working for justice, to making advances in technology that serve mankind.

Many examples from Scripture and the daily life of the Church illustrate how God has called us to participate in His work of salvation. A dramatic example of this, of course, is His choice of a particular young woman to bring the Savior into the world. As amazing as this sounds, the cosmos "hung in the balance" as God waited for Mary's "yes." (There is no guarantee that God would have given humanity another chance). So, in short, God has given us not only the extraordinary gift of redemption, but also the amazing opportunity and responsibility to participate in His salvific work. At Mass, this reality is highlighted by the fact that Jesus chose to use "the work of human hands," bread and wine, to make the Eucharist—and in the seemingly matter-of-fact gesture of people bringing up the gifts that will become the body and blood of Christ.

The bread and wine used, and the act of presenting them (along with baskets of our monetary gifts), are also symbolic. During the presentation of the gifts we should be offering all that we are and all "the good, the bad, and the ugly" of the past week to God. We should spiritually bring our entire lives to the altar together with the gifts that are brought in procession. We can do this by starting every morning with a simple prayer, offering our joys, works, sufferings, and our very selves to the Father in union with Jesus in the Eucharist. This makes worship "a new way of living our whole life, each particular moment of which is lifted up, since it is lived as part of a relationship with Christ and as an offering to God."[51]

This "lifestyle of worship" gives new meaning to everything, even what seems like the most senseless sufferings we have to face in life. When we offer things up to God, they become like powerful prayers, uniting us with Christ, and calling down grace for the salvation of the world (see Col 1:24).

Seen in this light, the Mass is not just an hour in our day. Rather, our whole day, our whole week, and our whole lives are taken up into this hour at the presentation of the gifts to become an offering to God the Father, through, with, and in Jesus Christ.[52]

82. **Why does the priest mix water and wine in the chalice during Mass?**

As the priest mixes a drop of water in with the wine before the consecration, he prays, "By the mystery of this water and wine may we come to share in the divinity of Christ, who humbled Himself to share in our humanity."

This prayer and action point to the amazing mystery that, just as the drop of water "lost" in the wine is transformed, in a sense, into wine, so our lives are transformed as they become joined to the life of God in the Eucharist. As St. Augustine says, "If you have received [the Eucharist] ... properly, you yourselves are what you have received." You are what you eat! Consequently, "not only have we become Christians, we have become Christ himself."[53] Or, in the words of St. Peter, we become "partakers of the divine nature" (2 Pt 1:4), sharing the "divinity of Christ who humbled himself to share in our humanity."

What does it mean to share in Christ's divinity? It means to be a child of God. ("See what love the Father has bestowed on us that we may be called the children of God. Yet so we are"—1 Jn 3:1.) A dog couldn't call a man "father" unless it had the heart and mind of a human. A human couldn't call God "father" unless God placed His own life, His own heart and mind, into that person. This is what happens through the sacraments of initiation (baptism, confirmation, and Eucharist). In baptism we become children of God, sharing in His life by the power of the Holy Spirit, who takes up a permanent dwelling in our souls. In confirmation, this life is brought to maturity in us, making us "adult" children of God, sharing in the mission of the Church. In the Eucharist this initiation is completed as we become one, even physically, with God. "God's whole life encounters us and is sacramentally shared with us" in the Eucharist.[54] Because of these sacraments that initiate us into the very life of God, we are able to know and love God as children know and love their father. Because of the sacraments of initiation we can say that we are "family" with the Trinity, sharing God's inner life, and, in a sense, that we have Christ's blood coursing through our veins. This amazing transformation, symbolized in the mingling of water and wine, is referred to in the Eastern rites of the Catholic Church and by our Orthodox brothers and sisters as "divinization."

83. Why does the priest wash his hands right before the consecration?

Shortly before the consecration the celebrant washes his hands: an altar server pours water over them and offers him a cloth with which to dry them. The priest does not do this just to make them clean. It is also a symbolic gesture: As he washes his hands he prays, "Lord, wash away my iniquity; cleanse me from my sin."

Pontius Pilate washed his hands when he turned Jesus over to the executioners as a sign that he bore no responsibility for His death. At Mass, the celebrant and the people both acknowledge their sins, which were the cause of our Savior's death, and ask forgiveness. The celebrant washes his hands because he is about to hold the sacred body and most precious blood of Christ at the consecration. This reflection is a reminder to all of us that we need to approach our Lord with "clean" hands and pure hearts. As the celebrant performs this hand-washing ceremony, we should pray for him and for ourselves.

84. Why do we sing "Holy, Holy, Holy" at every Mass?

This prayer, "Holy, Holy, Holy," traditionally called the *Sanctus* (Latin for "holy"), has been used in the liturgy since the very first days of Christianity. St. Clement of Rome, the fourth pope (believed to have been ordained by St. Peter himself), who was martyred in the year 101, mentions in his writings that this prayer was used at Mass.

The *Sanctus* is a song that comes straight from heaven. Isaiah had a vision of heaven, and the angels there were singing "Holy, holy, holy is the Lord of hosts ... all the earth is filled with his glory!" (Is 6:3). St. John also had a vision of heaven and wrote in the book of Revelation that he saw angels singing "Holy, holy, holy" (Rv 4:8). The Church's use of this prayer is quite intentional. At Mass we don't just imitate the worship of heaven, we actually join in it.

The priest introduces the *Sanctus* by praying: "And so, with all the choirs of angels in heaven we proclaim your glory and join in their unending hymn of praise." The priest could easily continue this prayer by himself, but the liturgy from the earliest days has the whole Church on earth break into song with him, joining in the worship of the Church in heaven that was going on long before the world began.

The last part of the *Sanctus*, "Blessed is he who comes in the name of the Lord; hosanna in the highest!" (Mt 21:9) was the praise that people were singing to Jesus as He entered Jerusalem for the last time, soon to be crucified and rise again. This is a fitting prayer of praise to set the stage for the re-presentation of the Paschal Mystery (the death, resurrection, and ascension of Jesus) in the Eucharist.

85. Why are bells rung by the altar server at certain times during Mass?

Before changes were introduced in the Mass following Vatican II, the words of consecration were pronounced by the priest in a very low voice—and in Latin. The faithful usually could not hear them. So the priest would hold up the consecrated host and the server would ring the bells to draw the attention of the congregation to Jesus Christ in the Eucharist. Because in the "new" Mass the words of consecration are prayed out loud and in the vernacular, the ringing of the bells is no longer required. But they are still permitted, and many parishes retain this wonderful tradition. It is a reverential way to help our wandering minds focus on the miracle happening before us on the altar.

86. Who is the priest "Melchizedek" mentioned during the Eucharistic prayer?

In Eucharistic Prayer I, one of the four prescribed Eucharistic prayers of the "new" Mass, we hear the priest say, "Look with favor on these offerings and accept them as once You accepted the gifts of Your servant Abel, the sacrifice of Abraham, our father in faith, and the bread and wine offered by Your priest Melchizedek."

While it is obvious that God the Father accepts the offering of God the Son in the Eucharist, these prayers remind us of the salvation history—and the priesthood—that finds its culmination in Jesus Christ. There have always been priests among God's people to offer sacrifices on their behalf. In Old Testament times, a man did not become a priest by applying for and attending the seminary. He needed to be a descendent of the priestly tribe of Israel, the Levites.

Melchizedek is a mysterious character who shows up in Genesis (14:18-20) to offer up a thanksgiving sacrifice of bread and wine on behalf of Abram (later to be named "Abraham" by God). Note that he offered a sacrifice of bread and wine—the original substances that a Catholic priest uses during Mass. Melchizedek was a priest and a king long before the Levites existed as a tribe. He then disappears as quickly as he appeared in Scripture.

St. Paul wrote to the Hebrews that Jesus, who was not a Levite, was "a priest forever in the order of Melchizedek." (This phrase, quoting Psalm 110:4 which prophecies about Christ, appears multiple times in Hebrews 5-7.). In doing this, Paul, who was writing to Jews, was showing them how Jesus fit into salvation history and that Jesus was a priest, not because of His family line, but by the power of God. He goes on in Hebrews to show how salvation history, and all priesthood, finds its culmination in Jesus Christ who is both the final high priest and the final atoning sacrifice.

All Catholic priests share in the one priesthood of Jesus Christ in the same way that He was a priest in the order of Melchizedek, not by being a descendent of a particular tribe, but by the power of God (see Heb 7:16) which transforms them through the sacrament of holy orders.

87. A few times during the Mass I have noticed the priest praying quietly. What is he saying?

Though he stands before us in the person of Christ (*in persona Christi*), the priest is still a sinful human being like you and me. Thus, he offers a few prayers for himself that are prescribed by the official text of the Mass, recognizing his own need for God's mercy:

+ As he washes his hands (i.e, the *ablution*) shortly before the consecration, he prays, "Lord wash away my iniquity; cleanse me from my sin."

+ Just before the consecration, as he pours a drop of water into the chalice full of wine, he prays, "By the mystery of this water and wine may we come to share in the divinity of Christ, who humbled Himself to share in our humanity."

✦ After the consecration, he places a small piece of the host into the chalice and says, "May this mingling of the body and blood of our Lord Jesus Christ bring eternal life to us who receive it." These are prayers he says quietly on behalf of the Church.

✦ Before he leads the congregation in praying, "Lord, I am not worthy to receive you ...," he prays a similar prayer for himself, asking for God's mercy and forgiveness.

✦ Finally, as he receives Holy Communion he prays, "May the body of Christ bring me to everlasting life ... May the blood of Christ bring me to everlasting life."

Perhaps during these times it would be good for us to offer up a silent prayer for our priests who, despite all their human weaknesses, have such an amazingly high calling.

88. What should we be doing when the priest is praying?

At Mass, we are not an audience but a congregation. There is a difference. An audience is there to be entertained, whereas a congregation is present to join in the sacrifice offered to God. We are called to full, active, and conscious participation in the Mass.[55]

But what does it mean to actively participate when the priest has a part to say and we don't? In these moments, active participation demands attentive listening and praying with the priest in our hearts. And, as the priest holds up Jesus in the Eucharist, we are called to be as Mary was at the foot of the Cross, cooperating in His offering. In our hearts, we should offer Jesus to God the Father with the priest for the salvation and sanctification of the world. And we should offer ourselves to the Father through Him, with Him, and in Him for the salvation of the world, too.[56]

This type of quiet, internal "activity" can be difficult because of the painfully short attention spans of our TV generation—but it is essential for praying well at the Mass.

89. Why does the priest drop a little piece of the host into the cup?

This is a symbol of both the Mystical Body of Christ, i.e., the Church, and the glorified body of Christ.

It is a symbol of the Mystical Body because, from the fourth century to about the tenth century, the pope (and, in some cases, a bishop) would send pieces of a host that he had consecrated around to his priests to be placed in the chalice and consumed at the Masses that they celebrated as a sign of their unity with him and with the universal Catholic Church. The little piece of host dropped into the chalice at Mass today harks back to this ancient practice.

It is also a symbol of the glorified body of Christ, because it reunites Christ's body and blood. In the Sacrifice of the Mass the separate consecration of the bread and wine symbolize the separation of Christ's body and blood at His death (although in reality He is entirely present in either form of Holy Communion).

The reuniting of His sacramental body and blood is a powerful reminder that, while the Mass is primarily sacrificial in nature, Jesus Christ is alive and well and is sharing His own divine life with us in the Eucharist. We are not consuming a dead body in Holy Communion, but the risen, glorified, and undivided body of our Savior.

As the priest drops the small piece of the host into the cup, he prays quietly, "May this mingling of the body and blood of our Lord Jesus Christ bring eternal life to us who

receive it." We are directly impacted by the power of Jesus'
risen life in the Eucharist. It is a life that is so powerful
that it defeated death. That is why Jesus, when talking
about the Eucharist in John 6, mentions "eternal life" more
than in any other single discourse, and why St. Ignatius
of Antioch, a disciple of St. John the Apostle who was
martyred around year 110, wrote that the Eucharist is "the
medicine of immortality and the antidote against death,
enabling us to live forever in Jesus Christ."[57]

When we live a life "fueled by Eucharist," we are no longer
living an average, ordinary life. We begin to partake in
"resurrection life," eternal life, here and now, or as Jesus
called it, "life to the full" (Jn 10:10)—even in the ordinary
events of every day.

**90. Why, during the Eucharistic prayer, does the priest
pray for God's angel to "take this sacrifice to your altar
in heaven"?**

The prayer from the Mass is: "Almighty God, we pray
that your angel may take this sacrifice to your altar in
heaven. Then, as we receive from this altar the sacred
body and blood of your Son, let us be filled with every
grace and blessing."[58]

This prayer is a powerful reminder that at the liturgy we
not only imitate, but actually participate in the worship of
the angels, saints, and our loved ones who have gone before
us. At the liturgy we are gathered with them around the
same God and Savior—Jesus Christ. You are never closer
to your departed loved ones than when you are at Mass, as
they are just on the "other side" of that altar.

The book of Revelation, the final book of the Bible, gives us a glimpse of heaven. While Revelation is full of future prophecy, it also filled with allusions to the worship taking place in heaven now—the heavenly liturgy. In Revelation we can see Sunday worship (1:10); an altar (8:3-4; 11:1; 14:18); priests (4:4; 11:15; 14:3;19:4); incense (5:8; 8:3-5); chalices (15:7; 21:9); the Gloria (15:3-4); Alleluia (19:1, 3, 4, 6); the words "Holy, Holy, Holy" (4:8); the word "Amen" (19:4; 22:21); the Lamb of God (5:6) and a marriage supper of the Lamb (19:6), among many other things. Do these things sound familiar? Revelation shows us the Mass from "the other side."[59]

Here is what the *Catechism* says about our union with heaven at Mass:

> In the earthly liturgy we share in a foretaste of that heavenly liturgy which is celebrated in the Holy City of Jerusalem toward which we journey as pilgrims, where Christ is sitting at the right hand of God, Minister of the sanctuary and of the true tabernacle. With all the warriors of the heavenly army we sing a hymn of glory to the Lord; venerating the memory of the saints, we hope for some part and fellowship with them; we eagerly await the Savior, our Lord Jesus Christ, until He, our life, shall appear and we too will appear with Him in glory (CCC 1090, quoting *Sacrosanctum Concilium*, no. 8).

The Mass is truly "a glimpse of heaven on earth."[60] No doubt, "our wounded freedom would go astray were it not already able to experience something of that future fulfillment" now.[61]

The song "I Can Only Imagine" recently became a hit. Sung by the group MercyMe, it speaks of the glory we will experience at the moment we get to heaven:

I can only imagine what it will be like, when I walk
by Your side ...
I can only imagine, what my eyes will see, when
Your Face is before me!
I can only imagine. I can only imagine.

Surrounded by Your Glory, what will my heart feel?
Will I dance for You, Jesus? Or in awe of You, be still?
Will I stand in Your presence, or to my knees will I fall?
Will I sing 'Hallelujah!'? Will I be able to speak at all?
I can only imagine! I can only imagine!

Thanks to the Mass, that moment is not left completely
to our imagination. We actually get a foretaste of heaven
here and now.

A five-year-old boy once asked his dad, "Is Jesus in our
hearts?"

"Yes, Ethan," his dad replied.

"Is it *heaven* in our hearts?"

This little boy's simple question reveals a profound truth:
wherever Jesus is, there is heaven. Our hearts long for
something bigger than this whole world can provide. In the
Eucharist we experience a foretaste of that love—heaven in
our hearts.

**91. Why do we offer prayers at Mass for people who
have died?**

Christians have always prayed for their beloved dead. This
is a continuation of the Jewish practice of praying for those
who have died. Prayer for the dead is mentioned explicitly
in the Bible in 2 Maccabees 12:46.

The practice in the Catholic Church is based on our belief in purgatory, the place where people go who die in the state of grace but are not yet ready for heaven because they need further purification before they can "fit in" with the company of the angels and saints (CCC 1031; also 1472 on the double effects of sin: separation from God and an unhealthy attachment to sin which needs purifying). It is a great gift of mercy that God should allow this time of purification after death to perfect us.

The Church consists of those who are on earth (traditionally called "the Church Militant"), those in purgatory ("the Church Suffering"), and those in heaven ("the Church Triumphant"). We are all one, together in Christ. In the words of the Vatican II document *Lumen Gentium*, "the union of the wayfarers (us on earth) with the brethren who have gone to sleep in the peace of Christ is not in the least weakened or interrupted, but on the contrary, according to the perpetual faith of the Church, is strengthened by communication of spiritual goods."[62]

When we are at Mass the entire Church is gathered around Christ together in worship, not only glorifying God, but benefiting from one another's presence and prayers. As we mentioned above, we are never closer to our loved ones who have died than at Mass. It is a fitting time to pray for them, as they surely are doing for us.

Sacred Scripture tells us very little about what purgatory is actually like. The Church traditionally refers to it as a purifying fire, alluding to imagery from 1 Corinthians 3:13 and 1 Peter 1:7 (see CCC 1031). We do know that we can help those suffering in purgatory to "speed up" their journey into the full presence of God by our prayers and sacrifices. If we do so, they will be wonderful allies and friends as saints in heaven.

Prayer for the "dead" (which is a relative term for Christians) is an act of charity, a work of mercy that we should perform regularly. It is also a beautiful way to practice reconciliation if there was an unforgiven grievance between you and one who has died.

(See CCC 1030-1032 for more about purgatory, and CCC 1471-1479 to learn about indulgences.)

92. During the Mass, we pray for the intercession of the saints. Doesn't the Bible forbid us from trying to contact the dead?

The Catholic Church has always taught that it is gravely wrong to conjure the spirits of the dead (see CCC 2116-2117, which cites Dt 18:10 and Jer 29:8).

The catch is that the saints of God aren't dead. In fact, they could not be any more alive! When the Church canonizes a saint, that is a proclamation that this person lived, and still lives in God, that we should look to him or her for an example in following Jesus (e.g., in 1 Corinthians 4:16, St. Paul says, "I urge you to imitate me"), and that we can ask for their intercession on our behalf. We can ask the living on this earth to pray to God for us, and we can ask the living in heaven to do the same. That is a far cry from witchcraft, conjuring spirits, and communing with the dead, all of which "conceal a desire for power over time, history, and, in the last analysis, other human beings" (CCC 2116).

Deuteronomy 34:7 is pretty clear that "Moses died." But in Matthew 17:1-6, we see Jesus talking with him and Elijah.

Although Moses had died physically, he was far from dead. He was alive in God, who is "not God of the dead but of the living" (Mk 12:27). When we pray to the saints, we are doing much the same thing as Jesus did in Matthew 17, and as Christians have done in honoring the saints and asking for their intercession since the very beginning of the Church.

God has brought us into a beautiful and living family. He is our Father, Mary is our spiritual Mother, and the saints are our big brothers and sisters who provide us with good example and are there to pray for us.

93. **Right before communion, we pray, "Lord I am not worthy to receive you." If we are not worthy, how can we receive Jesus' body and blood in communion?**

This prayer, "Lord, I am not worthy to receive you, but only say the word and I shall be healed," is based on a Scripture passage (see Mt 8:8) and expresses both our unworthiness to receive Jesus and our confidence in the power of His merciful love.

In the eighth chapter of Matthew's gospel, a Roman centurion approached Jesus asking Him to heal his servant who was dying. Jesus was about to go with him when the Roman stopped him, saying, "Lord, I am not worthy to have you enter under my roof, but only say the word and my servant will be healed." (In the Traditional Latin Mass, the Extraordinary Form of the Roman Rite, this prayer is repeated verbatim: *Domine, non sum dignus ut intres sub tectum meum. Sed tantum dic verbo ...*) He had total confidence in Jesus and knew that a word from Him was enough. Jesus was deeply moved by his faith and said, "Amen I say to you, in no one in Israel have I found such faith." As you might imagine, the Gospel account ends with the recovery of the centurion's servant.

The reality is that the centurion was not worthy to have Jesus come into his house, and we are not worthy to receive Jesus into our souls. Recognizing our unworthiness before God is essential to our relationship with Him. The same is true in human relationships. A good husband is forever grateful for the love of his wife. When she says, "I love you," could you imagine him saying, "Of course you do! I'm awesome!"? The words of our Lord, "This is my body, which is given up for you," are at least as profound as the words "I love you" from a spouse. We should respond in total humility and gratitude. We should be forever grateful for His unfathomable love for us and the power of His words, which heal us and enable us to receive Him. Though we are never worthy of Him, that He should love us and show us such mercy is an act worthy of Jesus, who is love and mercy itself.

94. Why do we sing at Mass? Has there always been music at Catholic worship?

As Pope Benedict XVI has said, "Music is a higher form of communication … when man comes into contact with God, mere speech is not enough … so he invites the whole of creation to become a song with him."[63]

Singing has been part of the Church's worship from the start. Check out Paul's words to the Colossians, written around the year 63: "Let the word of Christ dwell in you richly, as in all wisdom you teach and admonish one another, singing psalms, hymns, and spiritual songs with gratitude in your hearts to God" (Col 3:16).

Man did not invent music; God did. In the book of
Revelation, which gives us a snapshot of heavenly worship,
we see angels singing praise to God (see Rv 4:8). So there
was music in heaven long before the world was created.
At Mass, we join in the worship of heaven. Since there is
singing there, we should join in!

**95. Doesn't Vatican II say that the organ is the only instru-
ment we should use at Mass, along with Gregorian
chant? Isn't it wrong, then, to use other instruments
and styles of music during the liturgy?**

Vatican II reaffirms that the organ is the official
instrument of the Church and, because of this, it needs to
be "held in high esteem."[64] However, other instruments can
be used at the discretion of the bishop and of the pastor,
if they more effectively help people pray and enter into the
sacred mysteries at the Mass. Many Masses in Africa have
only drums and singing with no other instrument. (You
may want to Google "Missa Luba" for a beautiful CD of an
African Mass.) Similarly, many parishes in Latin America
use guitars, in part because they cannot afford organs.

The Magisterium of the Church gives guidelines for
which instruments can be used, but ultimately leaves the
judgment up to bishops in their given regions.[65] A key
guideline given in Vatican II's Constitution on the Liturgy,
Sacrosanctum Concilium, is that the instruments need to be
"suitable, or ...[able to be] made suitable, for sacred use."[66]
In other words, if the instrument and style of music used
is going to make everyone feel more like they are at a pub
or a nightclub, they are not suitable for Mass.

Another key point in this same document is that the
primary "instrument" at Mass is the human voice.[67] The

purpose of any instrument is to inspire and support the congregation in singing to God, because, as the oft-quoted remark of St. Augustine says, "He who sings, prays twice." The instrument should never drown out the voice or take center stage over the prayers being sung (e.g., a congregation pausing for an extended drum solo would not be appropriate for Mass).

Both authors have been at many Masses where the fine line of what is appropriate musically is crossed, and the "band" succeeds in packaging and delivering the sounds of a secular radio station instead of sacred music. This may draw an enthusiastic crowd, but to what is it drawing them? The music at Mass should help draw hearts and minds to a place that is not of this world—to the throne of God Himself.

Regarding Gregorian chant, your friend is confusing the word "only" with "especially." While the organ and chant are especially suitable for Mass, the Church is very clear that they are not the only instrument and form of music suitable for the Mass.

That being said, it seems that since Vatican II issued its Constitution on the Liturgy in 1963, we have gone to the opposite extreme. Chant is a beautiful form of music, yet it is hardly ever heard at Mass anymore. If chant is completely missing in action in a given diocese or country, "then somebody has made a mistake somewhere," according to Francis Cardinal Arinze, prefect of the Congregation for Divine Worship and the Sacraments. Pope Benedict XVI has recently reiterated the Church's encouragement of the use of Gregorian chant at Mass.[68]

Chapter 8

RULES AND REGS

96. How late can I be for Mass and still fulfill my Sunday obligation?

Many people hold to the traditional opinion that if one arrives after the Gospel reading, then the Mass does not count in fulfilling one's Sunday obligation. But the current *Code of Canon Law*, the official law of the Church, makes no such declaration. Common sense would tell us that if you miss the consecration, you have obviously "missed" the Holy Sacrifice of the Mass, but there is really no official Church teaching on "how late is too late." Perhaps this is because if there were, the Church might be seen as dismissing certain earlier parts of the Mass as unimportant. And perhaps this is because the Church wants to encourage us to be present from the entrance hymn.

If a husband plans to meet his wife at a restaurant for a fancy dinner date, does he ever ask, "Honey, how late can I come and still have it count as a date?" Not likely. A better question would be, "How *early* should I be for Mass?" or "How much time do I need to prepare myself to celebrate the most profound mystery of my faith?" Being late for Mass on a regular basis reveals a lack of proper reverence, and may even be something to bring to confession. That being said, everything from last-minute diaper changes to a traffic jam can make people late for Mass on occasion.

What about leaving early? Some have referred to the practice of exiting the church right after communion as "the Judas shuffle." Remember that Judas left the Last Supper "early" to go and betray Jesus. As a sign of respect, one should remain standing through the recessional hymn until the priest has processed down the aisle. Dashing out the door right after the final blessing may be a sign that, perhaps, we aren't aware of who we have just received in the Holy Eucharist.

We need to remember that Jesus is truly present within us until the natural qualities of the host dissolve. It is a good idea to remain for a moment or two in silent thanksgiving for the profound gift we have received. St. Thérèse of the Child Jesus has written, "Let us detain ourselves lovingly with Jesus and not waste the hour that follows Communion. It is an excellent time to deal with God and put before Him the matters that concern our soul ... As we know that good Jesus remains within us until our natural warmth has dissolved the bread-like qualities, we should take great care not to lose such a beautiful opportunity to talk with Him and lay our needs before Him." And St. Louis de Montfort said, "I would not give up this hour of Thanksgiving even for an hour of Paradise." While we aren't expected to pray for an hour, we certainly should not rush out the door. We will miss not only that focused time with Christ, but the final blessing from Him as well.

97. Why must we fast an hour before receiving communion? Did Catholics always have to do this?

Some of the Church's "rules and regulations" are actually not Church laws at all—they are part of Sacred Tradition, i.e., they are part of the deposit of faith revealed by Jesus Himself to the apostles. Sacred Scripture is a part of Sacred Tradition (see CCC 113, 120). The Mass, also found in Scripture, is another. Such things cannot be discarded or changed essentially because they are from God. However, rules such as the amount of time one needs to fast before communion are a part of Church discipline; they are not part of the deposit of faith. Disciplines can be (and have been) changed to help us better understand and live out our Catholic faith.

Prior to the 1950s, Catholics were required to fast from midnight; later, this was reduced to three hours prior to receiving communion. You can bet that early Masses were more packed back then! In 1966, Pope Paul VI reduced the Eucharistic fast to one hour. The rule is extremely simple: you cannot eat or drink anything (except water or medicine) for one hour before receiving the Eucharist. At a Sunday Mass, communion typically is not distributed until at least thirty minutes into the Mass. So if you stop eating thirty minutes before Mass begins, you are usually good to go. For a weekday Mass, communion is typically given within fifteen to twenty minutes following the start of Mass. It is best to play it safe and allow more time. If you do not make the hour fast, you should not receive. If it is Sunday you still fulfilled your obligation simply by attending Mass. As much as Jesus would like you to receive Him, you can bet that He is happier with your obedience to the Church.

We shouldn't worry about the bare minimum, though, and miss the point of this rule. It is a reminder of the importance of fasting, not just to prepare our bodies for the Eucharist, but as a spiritual sacrifice to God that purifies our souls by training us in self control and detachment from worldly comforts. Jesus did not command His followers to fast; He assumed that they would (see Mt 6:16). The Church has always seen fasting as essential to the spiritual life. In the words of St. Peter Chrysologus (406-450), "Prayer, mercy, and fasting: these three are one, and they give life to each other. Fasting is the soul of prayer, mercy is the lifeblood of fasting. Let no one try to separate them ... if you have only one of them or not all together you have nothing."

Fasting can be anything from eating bread and water for a day to depriving yourself of little things, such as dessert after dinner or mustard on your sandwich. On Good Friday and Ash Wednesday, the entire Church is asked to fast—at minimum, by only eating two small meals and one normal meal (a specific discipline to help us enter in to these holy days). Of course, those who are ill or elderly are not required to fast.

98. What happens if one receives communion in a state of mortal sin? Could he or she become physically ill?

St. Paul certainly recognized that receiving the Holy Eucharist unworthily could lead to illness. Look at what he wrote to the Corinthians:

> Whoever eats the bread or drinks the cup of the Lord unworthily will have to answer for the body and blood of the Lord. A person should examine himself, and so eat the bread and drink the cup. For anyone who eats and drinks without discerning the body, eats and drinks judgment on himself. That is why many among you are ill and infirm, and a considerable number are dying" (1 Cor 11:27-29).

Obviously St. Paul believed in the Real Presence of Jesus in the Eucharist, otherwise that is a pretty severe penalty! The problem that St. Paul was correcting was extreme: Many of those receiving the Eucharist did not recognize Jesus in the host and cup at all and were eating and drinking like pigs in the hopes of having a good meal; a strong case can be made, however, that living a double life by getting drunk and messing around with girls on Saturday night and then receiving Jesus Sunday morning is no less extreme. But will it actually make you sick to do so? It did in the early Church in Corinth, but the Holy Spirit was clearly acting in very overt and miraculous ways at that time to get the Church on the right track. That instance may have been necessary to solidify the Church's teaching that one needs to receive worthily. In any case, after almost two millennia of Church Tradition, the teaching is quite clear.

Today, we need to be just as concerned about making sure we receive the Lord in the state of grace. Like the Corinthians of old, we also need to heed the words of St. Paul who reminds us that one who receives unworthily "eats and drinks judgment on himself."

99. Why shouldn't we receive communion if we are in sin? Don't we need Jesus most then?

Receiving Holy Communion when we have only committed a venial sin is fine, as venial sin does not deprive us of God's sanctifying grace. Receiving Holy Communion when we are in mortal sin, though, is another matter; it actually is another sin. Why? In some sense our hearts are like a throne that Jesus sits on when He enters us in the Eucharist. Imagine covering that throne with dirt, alcohol, sexual images, and stolen goods, and then inviting Jesus to come and sit there. This would be a sacrilege. Likewise, we should at least clean the throne of our hearts of any dirt before inviting the King of the Universe to dwell there.

It would also be a pretense in our relationship with God to receive Him in the Eucharist when we are separated from Him by mortal sin. If you were to offend your girlfriend and then take her out on a date without apologizing or making amends, acting as if nothing were wrong, you would be building up a fake relationship. We should have more integrity than that. If there is a real division in a relationship, with God or others, it needs to be addressed and mended.

The Eucharist is not just step one in our relationship with God. It is the highest expression of our oneness with Him, just as the physical union of a husband and wife is the highest tangible expression of their oneness. If you have demolished your soul through mortal sin, the sacrament to rebuild it with is confession.

Don't misunderstand: you do need Jesus most when you are in mortal sin, and He is more anxious to receive you then than ever (see Mt 18:12—the Good Shepherd who would leave the rest of His flock just to look for you; also take a look at the beautiful parable of the Prodigal Son in Lk 15:11-24). This does not mean, though, that you should receive Him in communion then. Being in mortal sin should not cause you to miss Sunday Mass, because that is another sin. But before receiving Him in the Eucharist, go and meet him in the sacrament of reconciliation. He is waiting for you there.

If you are unsure whether or not you have committed a mortal sin, we would advise that you abstain from receiving communion and try to get to confession as soon as you are able. It is always better to err on the side of prudence—and reverence for the Eucharist—in this case. (For more about mortal sin and confession see questions 47 and 98.)

100. What if someone has a wheat allergy? Why can't the Church "bend the rules" and allow them to receive communion?

The Church received the sacraments from Jesus Christ and passes them down as a gift to every generation. The Church did not invent the sacraments. As a result, we need to follow the direction of Jesus as closely as possible. If we do not, we cannot presume that He will bless our efforts. At the Last Supper Jesus used wheat bread and grape wine. If we use something else, we risk having people think they are worshiping God when they are actually worshiping an unconsecrated piece of food. We cannot take that risk, so we follow Jesus' example and use what He used at the Last Supper.

Thanks to advances in science we are now able to make hosts with only .01% gluten, which still technically qualifies them as bread and makes it possible for most people with wheat allergies to receive. However, if a person's allergy is so severe that this is still too much gluten, he or she can receive communion from the cup alone (see question 28). As we have noted, if one receives only the precious blood, he or she receives the whole of Christ, body, blood, soul, and divinity. It would be better to deprive someone of the host than to risk placing an unconsecrated host before them as if it were Jesus.

But what if an allergic person is a recovering alcoholic? There are provisions made for that also. Unfermented wine (technically known as *mustum*) can be used. And what if that recovering alcoholic who is so allergic to gluten is badly allergic to grapes as well? In that one in a million case, sadly, that person cannot receive Holy Communion.

Here is an analogy from everyday life. Someone who is legally blind cannot be issued a driver's license. While this may be a hardship for the person, this is necessary for the safety of the road, i.e., for the common good of society. If the Church could permit someone with a wheat allergy to receive rice cakes for communion, they would do so. The pope and the bishops obviously want everyone to be able to receive Jesus, but they cannot change divine law in order to be accommodating on this point. They must preserve the integrity of the sacraments, particularly that of the Holy Eucharist; use of the proper matter of this sacrament—bread and wine—must be preserved. Otherwise, no valid consecration can occur.

101. How can a bishop claim the right to deny communion to anyone? Isn't that a matter between an individual and God?

We are not merely in a one-on-one, "Jesus and me" relationship with God. He redeemed us as a family, a people, a Church. Because of this, "sin is never a purely individual affair."[69] Our unity with God and our unity with His people are closely interrelated. If something is between you and God it is also between you and His Church. The Eucharist is a gift God makes of His own Son, given to us through the Church; it is not a "right" that anyone is entitled to. The Church's job is not only to give this precious gift to the world, but also to guard this gift—just as it is the Church's job to hand down and guard the "deposit of the Faith" (see CCC 84).

In keeping with this duty, the Church has always taught that no Catholic should receive communion when he is in mortal sin until he goes to confession. Then, when his relationship with both Jesus and His Church is restored, this communion can be "expressed in a return to the Eucharist."[70] So what to do about someone who is publicly known to have committed grave sin (e.g., the sin of scandal), such as a politician who has promoted abortion?

The policy of some bishops is to let people know what their disposition should be when receiving communion and to leave this decision to them—if effect, allowing priests to give communion to everyone who comes forward to receive. The individual may have converted and repented just before Mass, and the people giving out communion would have no way of knowing that.

Other bishops have taken the stance that public scandal demands public reform before the Church can allow the person to receive Holy Communion, so that the Church doesn't add to the scandal by seeming to condone it.

The pope, as head of the college of bishops, has left this pastoral decision in the hands of each diocesan bishop. As long as that is the case, it is the bishop's God-given task to decide how he will give and guard the gift of the Eucharist … and how he does this is between him and God. We should pray often for our bishops to have wisdom and strength in dealing with the many challenges they face every day. They carry a very heavy burden for God and for us.

"BONUS" QUESTIONS

102. Why can't non-Catholic Christians receive communion at Mass?

It all comes down to a question of belief. Even Catholics need to go through preparation before they receive Holy Communion for the first time so that they know— and truly believe in—what (rather, "who") they are receiving. Most Protestants do not share our belief in transubstantiation, i.e., that the bread and wine are truly and substantially changed into the body, blood, soul, and divinity of Jesus Christ (see questions 20-23 and especially question 26).

Although it may seem like a loving gesture to let non-Catholic Christians receive communion at Mass despite this difference of belief, it is not. In the words of St. Paul, we would be allowing them to "eat and drink judgment upon themselves" (see 1 Cor 1:29; see also question 98). Loving someone means doing what is good for them, not just what may feel good in the moment. Obviously, eating and drinking judgment upon themselves is not good for non-Catholics, nor does it honor Christ to encourage someone to receive the Eucharist when they think He is only *spiritually* present, that they are ultimately receiving just a "piece of bread."

But what about Orthodox Christians, who *do* believe in the Real Presence? If an Orthodox Christian cannot get to his own Church for some reason or is in danger of death, he may ask the priest and be granted permission to receive with us. (Confession and anointing of the sick are also available to non-Catholic Christians under the same circumstances.[71])

The reason is that the Eucharist is not the starting point of unity for Christians; it is the goal. Receiving Holy Communion implies that we are one in faith. If we did so, even though our sad divisions exist, we would be short-circuiting true ecumenism. What motivation would there be for us to work for that unity for which Jesus prayed to the Father shortly before His death—that His people might be one (see Jn 17). Division between Catholics and other Christians may be painful—and it should be.

103. Why can't someone who is divorced and remarried receive the Eucharist?

Marriage is a life-long bond based on a vow taken before God and witnessed by the Church. The Church takes this vow very seriously, because the bond of marriage provides the security necessary for the healthy development of children, the proper context for the unfolding of the married couple's life and love, and a strong foundation for a family to build on.

Marriage is also a sacrament, in which the married couple both symbolizes the love and devotion of Jesus to his Church (see Ephesians 5) and actually encounters that divine love in their relationship, which has become a vessel of sacramental grace.

Because marriage is a sign of the life-giving love and unity of Christ and the Church, it is deeply connected to and strengthened by the Eucharist: Jesus' body given up for us in love. Both authors of this book know of troubled marriages that have been saved by regular Eucharistic adoration by the spouses together. Because of the bond of marriage and the Eucharist, there is a deep inconsistency with divorce and the reception of Holy Communion.

Pope Benedict XVI recently re-affirmed the practice of denying the divorced and remarried Communion, writing that "their state and their condition of life objectively contradict the loving union of Christ and the Church signified and made present in the Eucharist."[72]

If someone is divorced and remarried, they should petition for an annulment. An annulment is not a divorce, which declares that a past marriage is dissolved. An annulment is a declaration, after extensive interviews and investigation, that the past marriage, for one reason or another, was not valid in the first place. In other words, it was never a sacramental marriage.

A divorced Catholic who is considering remarriage should initiate annulment proceedings before he or she even begins to date again. Marriage is a bond, and no one can give himself in marriage if he is not free from a previous bond. If you know a Catholic who is divorced and remarried, encourage him or her to call their local diocese to inquire about an annulment. It may be easier to get one than they thought, and when their status is clarified they won't have to deprive themselves any more of the Eucharist.

In the difficult situation in which a person is remarried, does not qualify for an annulment, and cannot remedy the situation, the Church cannot compromise her teaching on the Eucharist—but she does not condemn, either. As a compassionate Mother, she offers support and still considers these people children of God and of the Church.

In the same document referenced above, Pope Benedict XVI stated: "[T]he divorced and remarried continue to belong to the Church, which accompanies them with special concern and encourages them to live as fully as possible the Christian life through regular participation at Mass, albeit without receiving communion, listening to the word of God, eucharistic adoration, prayer, participation in the life of the community, honest dialogue with a priest or spiritual director, dedication to the life of charity, works of penance, and commitment to the education of their children."[73]

104. What should I do if the priest preaches something contrary to Catholic teaching or celebrates Mass in an unlawful way? What if just the music is bad or certain people distracting?

Usually, the Mass is celebrated with great reverence and fidelity to the regulations of the Church governing the liturgy (known as the *rubrics*). Unfortunately, you will sometimes encounter a celebration of the Mass that is less than it should be, whether as a result of careless preparation on the part of the priest or because of deliberate disregard for the authority of the Church. Pope Benedict XVI's apostolic exhortation *Sacramentum Caritatis*, which we have quoted extensively throughout this book, seeks to correct some of these abuses.[74]

A good approach is to write a letter to your pastor. Begin by thanking him for all his hard work, and then discuss the issues you are concerned about. If the problem is outright liturgical abuse (e.g. your pastor uses cookies and milk instead of bread and wine at Mass), it might be best to notify your bishop and let him know what is going on. You will probably be referred to the diocesan office of sacred worship or the vicar for priests. The Mass is not the property of your local pastor and he has no *right* to change the *rites*.

Something else to consider—if you think the music could be better or the lectors could proclaim the readings better, perhaps you are being called to help with those ministries. We tend to be quicker to curse the darkness than to light a candle. Perhaps that is because it is so much easier to complain than to do something about it.

All that being said, remember to go to Mass with the intention to pray, not critique. Then, even if some problem arises, you will be closer to Jesus by the closing song than you were at the entrance hymn.

NOTES

1   St. Augustine, *Confessions* 1,1,1: J.P. Migne, ed., *Patrologia Latina* 32, 659-661 (Paris, 1857-1866).

2   St. Thomas Aquinas, *Summa Theologica* I, 2, 3.

3   *Reader's Digest*, January 1963, p. 92

4   See Fr. Benedict Groeschel's *The cross at Ground Zero* (OSV, 2002) and *Arise from Darkness* (Ignatius Press, 1995).

5   See *Sacramentum Caritatis*, 89-90

6   See Lewis' book *Mere Christianity* for more on this argument.

7   His work, *The Testimony of the Evangelists*, was published in 1846.

8   *Sacramentum Caritatis*, no. 7

9   Ibid, no. 82

10 St. Augustine, *Confessions* 1,1,1: J.P. Migne, ed., *Patrologia Latina* 32, 659-661 (Paris: 1841-1855)

11 *Sacramentum Caritatis*, no. 2

12 St. Jerome, *Commentariorum in Isaiam libri xviii* prol.: J.P. Migne, ed., *Patrologia Latina* 24, 17b (Paris: 1841-1855).

13 *Sacramentum Caritatis*, no. 51; see also nos. 84 and 86.

14 See Ibid., no. 10

15 See *General Directory for Catechesis*, no. 51

16 Address of Pope John Paul II to youth in Kazakhstan, September 9, 2001.

17 See *Sacramentum Caritatis*, no. 66

18 Ibid., no. 33

19 Ibid., no. 70

20 For more about the meaning of *in persona Christi*, see questions 65, 72, and 87.

21 For more on Eucharistic miracles, check out the books *This is My body, This is My blood (Miracles of the Eucharist), Books I and II*, by Bob and Penny Lord (Journeys of Faith: 1-800-633-2484); to learn more about the miracle of Lanciano, go to the link: www.therealpresence.org/eucharst/mir/lanciano.html

22 For more information, see the letter of the Congregration for Divine
    Worship, issued May 29, 1969, granting the right to the bishops of each
    country to seek the permission of Rome for communion in the hand.
    Available at http://www.ewtn.com/expert/answers/communion_
    in_hand.htm. The United States Conference of Catholic Bishops
    (USCCB) was granted this permission on June 17, 1977, allowing
    communion in the hand for the first time in the United States.
23 *GIRM*, no. 160
24 *Sacramentum Caritatis*, no. 74; *Gaudium et Spes*, no, 26
25 Ibid., no. 37
26 *Sacramentum Caritatis*, no. 20
27 Ibid., no. 77
28 Ibid., no. 95
29 St. Justin, *Apologiae* 1, 65-67: J.P. Migne, ed., *Patrologia Graeca* (Paris,
    1857-1866) 6, 428-429.
30 *Sacramentum Caritatis*, no. 3
31 Vatican II, *Sacrosanctum Concilium*, no. 21
32 Ibid., no. 34
33 Ibid., no. 37
34 See *Sacramentum Caritatis*, no. 37-40
35 Ibid., no. 37
36 *Sacrosanctum Concilium*, no. 7
37 Ibid., no. 10
38 Ibid., Introduction
39 *GIRM*, no. 29
40 St. Josemaria Escriva, *The Way*, p. 537
41 John Paul II, *Dominicae cenae*, 3; quoted in CCC 1380
42 See *Sacramentum Caritatis*, no. 62
43 *GIRM*, no. 29
44 St. Ambrose *Letter* 22, no. 13
45 *Dedication of a Church*, no. 10
46 Vatican II, *Dei Verbum*, no. 11
47 Pope John Paul II, Homily at World Youth Day, 7/28/02
48 *Sacramentum Caritatis*, no 45
49 Pope Benedict XVI, *Sacramentum Caritatis*, no 49
50 Ibid., no. 47
51 Ibid., no. 71
52 "More than just statically receiving [Jesus at Mass], we enter into the
    very dynamic of his self-giving," *Sacramentum Caritatis*, no. 11
53 See *Sacramentum Caritatis*, no. 36
54 Ibid., no. 8

55 *Sacrosanctum Concilium*, no. 14

56 See *Sacramentum Caritatis*, no. 55

57 St. Ignatius of Antioch, *Letter to the Ephesians*, no. 20

58 This prayer is taken from Eucharistic Prayer I (also known as the "Roman Canon"), one of the four Eucharistic prayers found in the revised Roman Missal of 1969.

59 See Scott Hahn's book *The Lamb's Supper: The Mass as Heaven on Earth* (Doubleday, 1995) for a full list of liturgical references in Revelation and for more on this topic.

60 *Sacramentum Caritatis*, no. 35

61 Ibid., no. 30

62 *Lumen Gentium*, no. 49

63 Joseph Cardinal Ratzinger, *The Spirit of the Liturgy* (Ignatius Press, 2000), p. 136

64 *Musicam Sacram*, no. 62

65 The Fall 2007 meeting of the United States Conference of Catholic Bishops (USCCB) issued a document on liturgical music that offers guidance on this issue.

66 *Sacrosanctum Concilium*, no. 62

67 Ibid., no. 64

68 See *Sacramentum Caritatis*, no. 42

69 *Sacramentum Caritatis*, no. 20

70 Ibid.

71 See the *Directory for the Application of Principles and Norms on Ecumenism*, no. 129-131

72 *Sacramentum Caritatis*, no. 29

73 Ibid.

74 This entire encyclical is available on the Vatican website: www.vatican.va

ACKNOWLEDGMENTS

Many thanks to Michael J. Miller and Joseph Lewis, whose creative contributions helped improve many of the answers; to the staff and associates of Ascension Press, for appreciating the need for this project and helping see the book through to its completion; to the DesignWorks Group for yet another creative cover; and to all those priests whose profound reverence in celebrating the Mass has inspired teens to greater faith in and devotion to the most sublime mystery of the Holy Eucharist.

INDEX

(Listed by Topic and Question No.)

ABOUT THE AUTHORS

Matthew Pinto is the author of the best-selling question-and-answer book *Did Adam & Eve Have Belly Buttons?* (Ascension Press, 1998), co-author (with Jason Evert) of *Did Jesus Have a Last Name?* (Ascension Press, 2005), and creator of the *Friendly Defenders Catholic Flash Cards* series. Matt is co-founder of several Catholic organizations, including CatholicExchange. com and *Envoy* magazine, and the creator, with Jeff Cavins, of the *Amazing Grace* series of books. Matt and his wife, Maryanne, live in Pennsylvania with their six children.

Chris Stefanick is the director of youth, young adult, and campus ministry for the Archdiocese of Denver. He is a highly sought-after national speaker, and his dynamic keynotes, retreats, and chastity assemblies have inspired tens of thousands of young people to a deeper love for Jesus Christ and the Church. Chris regularly appears on Relevant Radio as the vice president of the Dead Theologians Society, and on *Catholic Answers Live* as a chastity speaker for the Pure Love Club. He and his wife, Natalie, live in Colorado with their four children.

More Best-Selling Resources for Teens

Did Adam & Eve Have Belly Buttons?
Matthew Pinto

With more than 200,000 copies sold, *Did Adam & Eve Have Belly Buttons?* is the number one book for Catholic teens. It offers today's young Catholic 200 clear and insightful answers to questions about the Catholic faith. The revised edition includes over 500 Bible and 800 *Catechism* references.

Imprimatur   *Price: $12.99*

"This is the most comprehensive question-and-answer book on the Catholic Faith that I've ever seen—and I've seen a lot of them! A to Z, it's all in here!"
–Mary Beth Bonacci
Author and Youth Speaker

"This book gives young people reliable answers to life's most important questions. Every teen should read it, and every parent of a teen should too."
–Mark Brumley
President, Ignatius Press

Did Jesus Have a Last Name?
Matthew Pinto & Jason Evert

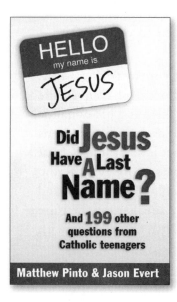

The long-awaited sequel to *Did Adam & Eve Have Belly Buttons?* Written by Matthew Pinto and Jason Evert, both of whom have extensive experience working with Catholic youth, this is a book your teen will want to read! Perfect for middle and high school religion classes, CCD, and youth groups.

Sample questions:

· How can we believe in a God we cannot see?

· How can Jesus be God and man at the same time?

· If God is good, why is there suffering and evil in the world?

· Is the Catholic Faith the only true religion?

Imprimatur   *Price: $12.99*

Who Should Use These Books:

- Teenagers
- High School religion teachers
- CCD Teachers

- Youth Ministers
- Parents of teens & pre-teens
- RCIA teachers & catechumens

Bulk Discounts Available
1-800-376-0520 • **www.AscensionPress.com**